D1020273

A NEW OWNER'S
GUIDE TO
DOBERMAN
PINSCHERS

JG-135

Overleaf: Doberman Pinscher adult and puppy photographed by Isabelle Francais.

Opposite page: Doberman Pinscher owned by Ron and Glenna Chedester.

The publisher wishes to acknowledge the following owners of the dogs in this book: Grace and Raquel Acosta, Ed and Nancy Asals, Nancy Basley, Ron and Glenna Chedester, Beverly Derr, Claire Henry, Carole Hoeker, HoMike Dobermans, Kathy and Mike Horniman, Arnold Jacobson, Keith and Pat Jarvis, Roslyn Jenkins, Nancy Gale Johnson, Nanci Kelley, Carl Kepler, A. and J. Marshall, Marion Muirhead, Steve Niles, Peter and Darlene Pavlovich, Stacy Perry, Carol Petruzzo, Ryanluxus Dobermans, Seecar Kennels, Judi and Don Shiffer, Lori Stevens, Gary and Faye Strauss, Truslove Kennels.

Photographers: Rick Beauchamp, Paulette Braun, Callea Photography, Isabelle Francais, Gay Glazbrook, Karen Taylor.

The author acknowledges the contribution of Judy Iby for the following chapters: Sport of Purebred Dogs, Identification and Finding the Lost Dog, Traveling with Your Dog, Health Care, Behavior and Canine Communication.

T.F.H. Publications, Inc.
One TFH Plaza
Third and Union Avenues
Neptune City, NJ 07753

This book has been published with the intent to provide accurate and authoritative information in regard to the subject matter within. While every precaution has been taken in preparation of this book, the publisher and author assume no responsibility for errors or omissions. Neither is any liability assumed for damages resulting from the use of the information herein.

ISBN 0-7938-2784-1

www.tfh.com

A New Owner's
Guide to
DOBERMAN
PINSCHERS

Faye Strauss

Contents

Mischievous puppies need to be taught the rules of the household.

There is nothing more adorable than a Doberman puppy.

The athleticism and grace of the Doberman Pinscher is evident.

The versatile Doberman can be trained to excel in obedience and as a guard dog.

The Doberman Pinscher loves to spend time with his family.

HISTORY of the Doberman Pinscher

Looking at the many varieties of dogs that exist today it is hard to believe they all have a common ancestor. Whether it is the tiny Chihuahua or the massive Great Dane, each and every one traces back to *Canis lupis*—the wolf. The wolf did not simply walk out of the forest and into man's home, the transition was long, slow and in reality, highly manipulated by man himself.

The journey from beast of the forest to the arrival of *Canis familiaris*, "man's best friend," began somewhere in the Mesolithic Period, over ten thousand years ago. At that time, simply providing food for himself and his family and staying out of harm's way was undoubtedly the Mesolithic human's major concern in life. This was especially difficult in that he had literally no tools to assist him in his pursuits.

There are few breeds more majestic than the Doberman Pinscher.

Anything that might reduce early man's burdensome existence was undoubtedly looked upon with great interest. Observation of the wolf might well have taught man some effective hunting techniques that he was capable of employing himself. Additionally, many of the wolf's social habits could have seemed strikingly familiar as well. The association grew from there.

As time passed, wolf families found an easily obtained food source in man's discards and man realized certain descendants of the increasingly domesticated wolves could be advantageously selected to assist in hunting and other survival pursuits. The wolves that could assist in satisfying the unending human need for food and those courageous enough to afford protection from predators were, of course, most highly prized.

The wolves that performed any function that lightened early human existence were cherished and allowed to breed. Those that were not helpful or whose temperament proved incompatible were driven away.

With the passing of time humans realized they could manipulate breedings of these domesticated wolves so that the resulting offspring were more proficient in particular areas than preceding generations. As human populations developed a more sophisticated lifestyle, they also thought up new ways in which the wolves could be of assistance. Customizing the evolving wolves to suit growing human needs was the next step. They became hunting wolves, guard wolves, and herding wolves. The list of useful duties grew and grew. As centuries passed certain of these beasts of the forest had become full-time companions to man and thus *Canis familiaris*, the dog, was born. Ironically, the wolf, the actual ancestor of these animals, became enemy to both man and dog.

The versatile Doberman is equally at home on the land or sea.

ROMANS CLASSIFY THE BREEDS

Documentation of controlled breeding practices by Roman writers can be found as early as the first century AD. The Romans actually broke down the various types of dogs into six general classifications very similar to the "variety groups" used as a classification method by the American Kennel Club today. Two thousand years ago Roman writers talked of "house guardian dogs, shepherd dogs, sporting dogs, war dogs, scent dogs, and sight dogs."

Many of our modern breeds can trace their ancestry directly back to members of these early groups. Other breeds were developed by combining two or more individuals from these different categories to create yet another breed.

BIRTH OF THE DOBERMAN PINSCHER

Most dog breeds were created to accomplish a particular task, albeit at times nothing more than companionship. By and

The Doberman's high degree of intelligence, coupled with his fearless and protective nature, make him an ideal candidate for police work.

large, however, the vast majority of breeds owe their existence to man's need for assistance. Breeds were created to help in the pastures, on the hunt, and to serve as draught animals. Man also realized the dog was capable of offering him protection from harm.

The German, Herr Karl Friedrich Louis Dobermann, was one such individual who firmly believed this to be true. Thus, in the 1880s, he embarked upon a plan to produce a breed of dog that could indeed protect him as he performed his duties as a night watchman and tax collector.

Louis Dobermann resided in Apolda, Germany, a town in the eastern province of Thueringen. In addition to his role as tax collector, he was also keeper of the local dog pound to which any stray dog captured on the town's streets was sent.

This gave the gentleman access to any type of dog he might need in order to create the "wonder breed" he had decided to produce.

Aside from his need for protection, Dobermann was an admirer of the larger, more aggressive dogs that found their way to the shelter he managed. The end result in his project reveals he sought to produce a fearless dog of enough size to present an imposing picture, but yet not so large as to become difficult to manage. His canine experience no doubt made it obvious that a smooth-coated dog required far less work than one with luxuriant furnishings. The dog would certainly need to be alert and agile and possess unquestionable stamina, as it would have to accompany him on his arduous rounds of the city.

Records indicate a nondescript breed known as the German Pinscher existed during Louis Dobermann's time. The breed was of good size, very alert and had a very aggressive attitude. This was the dog upon which Herr Dobermann chose to establish his own breed. To this foundation, Dobermann added the blood of the Rottweiler and the old German Shepherd Dog (a dog differing greatly from the German Shepherd as we know it today). He used the Rottweiler because of its great courage, massive size, and tracking ability. The resulting progeny were medium-sized, black, heavy for their size, and aggressive. They became known as "Dobermann's dogs." While this cross produced a dog that possessed the mental qualities he considered of consequence, it appears Herr Dobermann was not entirely satisfied with the appearance of his dogs.

It is generally agreed that the Manchester Terrier, then a much larger breed than it is today, was introduced into the gene pool. From this cross came the smooth, lustrous coat and

A well-trained and well-socialized Doberman Pinscher will lay down his life to protect those he loves.

the distinctive black and tan markings. The Manchester also contributed a certain elegance and style the previous generations had not possessed. It appears that Herr Dobermann sought to combine power with a sleek and agile appearance because yet another cross was made—this time to the Greyhound. This also brought more stamina and speed to the developing breed.

Conscientious breeders are responsible for bringing forth the Doberman's best physical qualities as well as their good temperament and stability.

Herr Otto Goeller, another Apolda resident, was Dobermann's protégé. He continued on with his mentor's breeding and developmental plans long after the death of Dobermann in 1894, and it is Goeller who is credited by many as the true architect of the breed.

Goeller organized the National Dobermann Pinscher Club in 1899 and shortly thereafter, he and his committee members wrote the first breed standard. The German Kennel Club granted the breed official recognition to the club immediately thereafter.

Though recognition was immediate and appreciation for the abilities of the breed ran high, even the staunchest of the breed's supporters were still not satisfied with the breed's appearance. A critique written after a major entry show revealed, "The Doberman was still coarse throughout, his head showed heavy cheeks and the dogs had too wide and too French fronts; in coats the dogs were too long and wavy, especially long on the neck and shanks. A lot of dogs were built too heavy, appearing more like a Rottweiler."

With each passing year, however, more improvement and uniformity was achieved. Goeller remained the dominant breeder, and by the early 1900s, he did a great deal of winning with an excellent female named Ulrich's Glocke v. Thueringen.

Glocke produced two sons, Graf Belling v. Thueringen and the Sieger, Hellegraf v. Thueringen. Hellegraf v. Thueringen was considered to be the greatest sire produced in the breed not only to that time but for many years after. The two brothers were used heavily at stud but it was Hellegraf in particular that passed on a nobility and elegance that was to achieve international admiration for the breed.

The years of World War I nearly cost the Doberman Pinscher his existence. Lack of food and the adverse economic conditions in Germany forced many of the breed's devotees to put their dogs down to avoid inevitable starvation.

Had the German army not employed some Dobermans as part of the war effort, there is no doubt whatsoever that the breed would have become extinct in his homeland. Even the close of the war did little to restore any strength to the breed as economic conditions remained at survival level only.

Fortunately, some of the best dogs that had been saved were exported to other countries. They brought high prices, particularly those sold to the United States, but the fact remains that their sale only served to further decimate the already depleted breeding stock in Germany.

THE DOBERMAN IN AMERICA

The first Doberman Pinschers reached America in 1908. In that same year, Theodore F. Jaeger and his partner, W. Dobermann (said to be a descendent of the breed's founder) established a kennel that was granted the kennel name "Doberman" by the American Kennel Club. The kennel produced the breed's first American champion, Doberman Dix.

The first official meeting of America's Doberman Pinscher fanciers was held in New York City in 1921 and the Doberman Pinscher Club of America was founded in the same year by

George H. Earle III. American interest in the breed was growing by leaps and bounds. The big winners in the breed, however, were European imports—the few remaining good ones from

In comformation showing, handlers will stack their dogs to show to their best advantage.

Germany and the rest from the European countries to which Germany's best stock was sent.

Hunter, herder, draught dog or companion—there seems to be no limit to a Doberman's capabilities.

In 1928, however, at the Rhode Island Kennel Club Show, Ch. Big Boy of White Gate helped turn the tide by taking the first all-breed Best In Show for an American-bred Doberman.

The Doberman had established itself as a breed to be reckoned with in America's show rings as the '20s came to a close. Much of the breed's popularity was due to influential breeder-exhibitors such as Francis F. H. Fleitmann of Westphalia Kennels fame, who had imported Europe's finest Dobermans and used the imports intelligently to breed outstanding dogs himself.

One of Mr. Fleitmann's imports was the German Seiger bitch Ch. Jessy von der Sonnenhohe. She was both a marvelous show dog and an outstanding producer both in Germany and in America. "Jesse" had produced offspring prior to leaving Germany and they did exceedingly well there. One of her winning sons in Germany was Ch. Ferry von Raufelsen from a litter bred by Wilheim Rothfessy.

Ferry was brought to America in 1939 by Mrs. Geraldine Dodge of Geralda Kennels fame. Three weeks after his arrival in America, Ferry became the first of his breed to be declared Best In Show at the famed Westminster Kennel Club. Making the historic award was the highly respected judge George S. Thomas.

Thomas's critique of Ferry was extremely positive but concluded with the statement that the only thing he didn't like about Ferry was the fact that he could not touch the dog! A trained attack dog, Ferry's extremely aggressive temperament was everything Germany held in high regard, but it was a character that would haunt the breed for many years to come.

Originally bred to be an inherently aggressive attack dog, today's Doberman Pinschers must be professionally trained to carry on this tradition.

Ferry did a significant amount of winning and was heavily bred too. Unfortunately for the breed, Ferry passed along his fiery temperament along with the sterling qualities of conformation for which he was noted. Frequent attacks on humans by his offspring in particular, and the breed in general, earned them a very unsavory reputation that the breed was forced to live with for many years. Dedicated breeders worked diligently to improve this aspect of their breed. Unfortunately, the second World War's United States Marine Corps' claim that their "devil dogs" were the "toughest, most feared dogs in the world" did nothing to change the public opinion of the Doberman.

There is not enough that can be said in praise of American Doberman Pinscher breeders. It is through their concentrated and cooperative efforts that the best of the breed's physical and mental qualities have been preserved while the character deficiencies of the early imports have been eliminated.

This Doberman, bred by Truslove Kennels, is being carefully trained as a guard dog.

Few dogs did more to help repair the Doberman's reputation than Ch. Rancho Dobe's Storm

bred by Mr. & Mrs. Brint Edwards, owners of the Rancho Dobe Kennels in Van Nuys, California. Storm, who was owned by Mr. and Mrs. Len Carey, came onto the scene in 1949. He was one of 13 puppies actually born on December 13. (To break the "jinx" the litter was registered as having been whelped on December 12!)

There was nothing but trouble at the beginning. Nearly all of the litter was lost and Storm was the only male to survive. It was this single male's destiny to carry on the strange association with the number 13.

Storm was the Edwards' 13th homebred champion, and he became the 13th Doberman that handler Peter Knoop would handle to his championship. Storm's catalog number was 13 at the Westminster show at which he won his first Best In Show, and that show was his 13th time in the show ring. And it was exactly 13 years since the day his grandfather, Ch. Ferry v. Raufelsen of Giralda, became the first Doberman to win Best In Show at Westminster!

The athletic Doberman Pinscher has the ability to excel at many different activities. This Dobe clears the bar jump with graceful ease.

The Doberman makes an excellent family pet and, when properly socialized, gets along wonderfully with children. Charlene Ryan with her friend Romeo.

In the end, the number 13 was to provide nothing but great success to "the Storm dog." His record in the ring was remarkable: shown a total of 26 times, he won 17 all-breed Bests In Show plus two Specialty Bests In Show. He was chosen Best Working Dog a total of 22 times. But it was Storm's sterling temperament that was to have such a profound effect upon the breed. He captured America's attention and the public took this magnificent animal to their hearts.

Storm was the subject of international newsreels and enjoyed press coverage never before afforded to a dog of any breed. This coverage included a feature in *Life Magazine* with photographs by several world-famed photographers. Royal Daulton fashioned one of their famous ceramic models from his likeness. Storm and his owner Shirley Carey were part of a national promotion for Lucky Strike cigarettes. *Esquire* magazine called Storm "the greatest thing on four canine legs."

Storm died in 1960 but not before turning the tide for America's opinion of the breed. The dreaded "devil dog" was earning a place as one of America's most respected companions.

STANDARD of the Doberman Pinscher

General Appearance—The appearance is that of a dog of medium size, with a body that is square. Compactly built, muscular and powerful, for great endurance and speed. Elegant in appearance, of proud carriage, reflecting great nobility and temperament. Energetic, watchful, determined, alert, fearless, loyal and obedient.

Size, Proportion, Substance—
Height at the withers: *Dogs* 26 to 28 inches, ideal about 27 $^1/_2$ inches; *Bitches* 24 to 26 inches, ideal about 25 $^1/_2$ inches. The height, measured vertically from the ground to the highest point of the withers, equalling the length measured horizontally from the forechest to the rear projection of the upper thigh. Length of head, neck and legs in proportion to length and depth of body.

Author Faye Strauss pictured winning Best in Show with Ch. Sherluck's Good As Gold.

Head—Long and dry, resembling a blunt wedge in both frontal and profile views. When seen from the front, the head widens gradually toward the base of the ears in a practically unbroken line. *Eyes* almond shaped, moderately deep set, with vigorous, energetic expression. Iris, of uniform color, ranging from medium to darkest brown in black dogs; in reds, blues, and fawns the color of the iris blends with that of the markings, the darkest shade being preferable in every case. *Ears* normally cropped and carried erect. The upper attachment of the ear, when held erect, is on a level with the top of the skull.

Top of skull flat, turning with slight stop to bridge of muzzle, with muzzle line extending parallel to top line of skull. Cheeks flat and muscular. *Nose* solid black on black dogs, dark brown on red ones, dark gray on blue ones, dark tan on fawns. Lips lying close to jaws. Jaws full and powerful, well filled under the eyes.

Teeth strongly developed and white. Lower incisors upright and touching inside of upper incisors—a true scissors bite. *42*

correctly placed teeth, 22 in the lower, 20 in the upper jaw. Distemper teeth shall not be penalized. *Disqualifying Faults:* Overshot more than $^3/_{16}$ of an inch. Undershot more than $^1/_8$ of an inch. Four or more missing teeth.

Neck, Topline, Body—*Neck* proudly carried, well muscled and dry. Well arched, with nape of neck widening gradually toward body. Length of neck proportioned to body and head. *Withers* pronounced and forming the highest point of the body. Back short, firm, of sufficient width, and muscular at the loins, extending in a straight line from withers to the slightly rounded croup.

Chest broad with forechest well defined. *Ribs* well sprung from the spine, but flattened in lower end to permit elbow clearance. *Brisket* reaching deep to the elbow. *Belly* well tucked up, extending in a curved line from the brisket. *Loins*

Ear cropping is purely cosmetic and a matter of choice on the part of the owner. Seecar Hot Enchilada sports the uncropped look.

Judi and Don Shiffer's six-month-old puppy gives every promise of maturing into a lovely show prospect.

wide and muscled. *Hips* broad and in proportion to body, breadth of hips being approximately equal to breadth of body at rib cage and shoulders. *Tail* docked at approximately second joint, appears to be a continuation of the spine, and is carried only slightly above the horizontal when the dog is alert.

Forequarters—*Shoulder Blade* sloping forward and downward at a 45-degree angle to the ground meets the upper arm at an angle of 90 degrees. Length of shoulder blade and upper arm are equal. Height from elbow to withers approximately equals height from ground to elbow. *Legs* seen from front and side, perfectly straight and parallel to each other from elbow to pastern; muscled and sinewy, with heavy bone. In normal pose and when gaiting, the elbows lie close to the brisket. *Pasterns* firm and almost perpendicular to the ground. Dewclaws may be removed. *Feet* well arched, compact, and catlike, turning neither in nor out.

Hindquarters—The angulation of the hindquarters balances that of the forequarters. *Hip Bone* falls away from spinal column at an angle of about 30 degrees, producing a slightly

Dobermans possess distinctive rust-colored markings above each eye, and on the muzzle, throat, chest, legs and feet.

rounded, well filled-out croup. *Upper Shanks* at right angles to the hip bones, are long, wide, and well muscled on both sides of thigh, with clearly defined stifles. Upper and lower shanks are of equal length. While the dog is at rest, hock to heel is perpendicular to the ground. Viewed from the rear, the legs are straight, parallel to each other, and wide enough apart to fit in with a properly built body. Dewclaws, if any, are generally removed. *Cat feet* as on front legs, turning neither in nor out.

    Coat—Smooth-haired, short, hard, thick and close lying. Invisible gray undercoat on neck permissible.

    Color and Markings—*Allowed Colors:* Black, red, blue, and fawn (Isabella). *Markings:* Rust, sharply defined, appearing above each eye and on muzzle, throat and forechest, on all legs and feet, and below tail. White patch on chest, not exceeding

$^1/_2$ square inch, permissible. *Disqualifying Fault:* Dogs not of an allowed color.

Gait—Free, balanced, and vigorous, with good reach in the forequarters and good driving power in the hindquarters. When trotting, there is strong rear-action drive. Each rear leg moves in line with the foreleg on the same side. Rear and front legs are thrown neither in nor out. Back remains strong and firm. When moving at a fast trot, a properly built dog will single-track.

Temperament—Energetic, watchful, determined, alert, fearless, loyal and obedient. *The judge shall dismiss from the ring any shy or vicious Doberman.*

These newborn littermates demonstrate the black and red colors found in the Doberman Pinscher.

Shyness: A dog shall be judged fundamentally shy if, refusing to stand for examination, it shrinks away from the judge; if it fears an approach from the rear; if it shies at sudden and unusual noises to a marked degree.

Viciousness: A dog that attacks or attempts to attack either the judge or its handler, is definitely vicious. An aggressive or belligerent attitude towards other dogs shall not be deemed viciousness.

Faults

The foregoing description is that of the ideal Doberman Pinscher. Any deviation from the above described dog must be penalized to the extent of the deviation.

DISQUALIFICATIONS

Overshot more than 3/16 of an inch, undershot more than 1/8 of an inch. Four or more missing teeth. Dogs not of an allowed color.

Approved February 6, 1982
Reformatted November 6, 1990

CHARACTERISTICS of the Doberman Pinscher

All puppies are cuddly and cute. Even the Doberman baby with his floppy ears and oversized feet has a special charm that is hard to resist. There is nothing more seductive than a litter of little puppies nestled together, sound asleep, one on top of the other. But in addition to being cute, puppies are living, breathing and very mischievous little creatures, and they are entirely dependent upon their owner for everything once they leave their mother and littermates. Further, the innocent-appearing and dependent little Doberman puppy quickly becomes a dynamo of energy whose adolescent hormones continuously rage and inspire relentless activity.

It's hard to resist a sweet Doberman Pinscher puppy, but make sure your decision to get a dog is a carefully considered one.

Buying a dog, especially a Doberman puppy, before someone is absolutely sure they want to make that commitment can be a serious mistake. The prospective dog owner must clearly understand the amount of time and work involved in the ownership of any dog. Failure to understand the extent of the commitment involved is one of the primary reasons there are so many unwanted canines that end their lives in an animal shelter.

Before anyone contemplates the purchase of a dog there are

some very important conditions that must be considered. One of the first important questions that must be answered is whether or not the person who will ultimately be responsible for the dog's

This adorable Brookmeadow Doberman pup is all ears!

care and well being actually wants a dog.

If the prospective dog owner lives alone, all he or she needs to do is be sure that there is a strong desire to make the necessary commitment dog ownership entails. In the case of family households it is vital that the person who will ultimately be responsible for the dog's care really wants a dog. In the average household, mothers, even working mothers, are most often given the additional responsibility of caring for the family pets, even though today mothers are out in the workplace as well. All too often they are saddled with the additional chores of feeding and trips to the veterinarian although getting a dog originally was a family project.

Pets are a wonderful method of teaching children responsibility. The enthusiasm that inspires children to promise anything in order to have a new puppy may

Supervised visits with children can do wonders when it comes to socializing a young puppy. Andrew, Rob and Scott make friends with Dobe pup Ed.

quickly wane. Who will take care of the puppy once the novelty wears off? Does that person want a dog?

Desire to own a dog aside, does the lifestyle of the family actually provide for responsible dog ownership? If the entire family is away from home from early morning to late at night, who will provide for all of a puppy's needs? Feeding, exercise, outdoor access and the like cannot be provided if no one is home.

A fenced-in yard is very important if you are thinking of bringing a Doberman Pinscher into your family.

Another important factor to consider is whether or not the breed of dog is suitable for the person or the family with which it will be living. Some breeds can handle the rough and tumble play of young children. Some cannot. On the other hand, some dogs are so large and clumsy, especially as puppies, that they could easily and unintentionally injure an infant.

Then too, there is the matter of hair. A luxuriously coated dog is certainly beautiful to behold, but all that hair takes care. In the case of a Doberman there is no long hair to groom, but shorthaired dogs also shed their coats in the home. While the longer hair is more noticeable, the short hairs of the Doberman coat can prove to be extremely difficult to pick up.

As great as claims are for any breed's intelligence and trainability, remember the new dog must be taught every household rule that he is to observe. Some dogs catch on more quickly than others and puppies are just as inclined to forget or disregard lessons as young children.

CASE FOR THE PUREBRED DOG

While all puppies are cute, not all puppies grow up to be particularly attractive adults. What is considered beauty by one person is not necessarily seen as attractive by another. It is almost impossible to determine what a mixed breed puppy will look like as an adult. Nor will it be possible to determine if the mixed breed puppy's temperament is suitable for the person

These proud owners pose with their new Doberman puppy.

or family who wishes to own him. If the puppy grows up to be too big or too active for the owner, what then will happen to him?

Size and temperament can vary to a degree even within a purebred breed. Still, selective breeding over many generations has produced dogs giving the would-be owner reasonable assurance of what the purebred puppy will look and act like as an adult. Points of attractiveness completely aside, this predictability is more important than one might think.

A person who wants a dog to go along on those morning jogs or long-distance runs is not going to be particularly happy with a lethargic or short-legged breed. Nor is the fastidious housekeeper, whose picture of the ideal dog is one that lies quietly at the feet of its master by the hour and never sheds, going to be particularly happy with the shaggy dog whose temperament is reminiscent of a hurricane.

Purebred puppies will grow up to look like their adult relatives and by and large they will behave pretty much like the rest of their family. Any dog, mixed breed or not, has the potential to be a loving companion. A purebred dog offers reasonable assurance that he will not only suit the owner's lifestyle, but the person's esthetic demands as well.

WHO SHOULD OWN A DOBERMAN PINSCHER?

Just as a prospective buyer should have a check list to lead him or her to a responsible breeder, so do good breeders have a list of qualifications for the buyer. These are just a few of the "musts" for a prospective Doberman owner:

Dobermans are very social animals and thrive when allowed to spend time with their families.

1. The buyer must have a fenced yard.

2. The dog must live indoors with his owner.

3. Young, single or unsettled people can be poor candidates. The future spouse invariably wants a different breed or may be afraid of a Doberman.

4. Children should be over four years of age except in very special cases.

5. *Everyone* in the family must want a Doberman. Both the husband and wife must be interviewed to determine their desire to own a Dobe.

6. The buyer must be financially able to provide proper veterinary and home care.

7. No Doberman to parties who are interested in mass producing Dobes or operating an indiscriminate "stud factory."

8. The buyer must clearly understand the Doberman demands affection, attention, kindness, and firmness.

The Doberman Pinscher is most definitely not a breed for everyone! As sturdy a constitution as the Doberman may have and as high as his tolerance for discomfort might be, a Dobe is completely incapable of withstanding being struck in anger. This devastates and confuses the Doberman, and if subjected to treatment of this nature on a continuing basis, it can turn even the most amiable youngster into a neurotic and unpredictable adult.

The Doberman needs a "pack leader" to help him achieve the potential that he is born with. The properly trained Dobe will reward his owner with years of irreplaceable companionship and devotion.

A young Dobe must start understanding household rules from the first moment he comes into your home. It will take patience, love and a firm but gentle and unrelenting hand to accomplish this. Even the youngest Dobe puppy understands the difference between being corrected and being abused.

Someone who needs a dog that does well living outdoors with minimal owner interaction should in all fairness look to another breed. The Dobe must have constant human companionship and social interaction, not only with his owner, but with all kinds of people and other dogs. This is essential to the well-being of the breed.

CHARACTER OF THE DOBERMAN PINSCHER

A good part of the Doberman Pinscher's more obvious essence is in his bold and alert attitude. Beneath those surface characteristics, however, are the more subtle and telling things that really make the Doberman the unique breed that he is.

Faithful and fearless, Doberman courage is legendary. Once the Doberman has become a member of the human family, he is totally committed. The Doberman's devotion cannot be compromised. It makes no difference to the Dobe if time is spent hiking the hills, walking the beach or quietly listening to music. The breed lives to be included in everything his owner and owner's family does.

Those who have owned a Doberman are aware of the breed's inherent intelligence and keenness. Doberman owners know their dog would happily lay down his life for them.

The Doberman possesses a particular quality that can be attributed to few other breeds. The late Peggy Adamson, universally hailed as one of the breed's great authorities, described this quality as "honesty." It is observed in the

Doberman's open and direct look and apparent in his unequivocal loyalty.

This is not to say the Doberman is purely dour and serious. On the contrary, with his owners the Dobe can be a true clown—a funny dog possessed with a great sense of humor. The Dobe enjoys nothing more than being able to entertain his owners. It is that "secret" side of the Doberman that he reserves only for those he loves.

The Doberman is born with the potential to manifest all of these marvelous qualities but the new owner or prospective owner must understand one thing—none of these characteristics develop if the Doberman is not handled with respect and authority.

The Doberman's alert intelligence, loyalty and energy make him an outstanding service dog for the physically challenged.

SELECTING the Right Doberman for You

Once the prospective Dobe owner satisfactorily answers all the questions relating to responsible ownership, he or she will undoubtedly want to rush out and purchase a puppy immediately. Do not act in haste. The purchase of any dog is an important step since he will live with you for a great many years. In the case of a Doberman Pinscher this could easily be 10 or 12 years. You will undoubtedly want the dog you live with for that length of time to be one you will enjoy.

It is extremely important that your Doberman is purchased from a breeder who has earned a reputation over the years for consistently producing dogs that are mentally and physically sound. Not only is a sound and stable temperament of paramount importance in a large breed of this kind, but there are also a number of diseases that exist in the breed that good breeders are concerned with and will not breed dogs that are known to be inflicted. Unfortunately, the buyer must indeed beware that there are always those who are ready and willing to exploit a breed for financial gain, with no thought given to his health or welfare or to the homes in which the dogs will be living.

It is not a good idea to give a puppy as a gift, but if you do, make sure the recipient is ready and willing to take on the commitment of owning a Doberman.

The only way a breeder can earn a reputation for producing quality animals is through a well-thought-out breeding program in which rigid selectivity is imposed. Selective breeding is aimed at maintaining the virtues of a breed and eliminating genetic weaknesses. This process is time consuming and costly. Therefore, responsible Doberman breeders protect their investment

A puppy makes a wonderful companion for a child and caring for a pet is a great way to teach a child responsibility.

Your Dobe will have a good start in life if his parents are healthy and well adjusted. If possible, try to see the dam and littermates of the puppy you are considering.

by providing the utmost in prenatal care for their brood matrons and maximum care and nutrition for the resulting offspring. Once the puppies arrive, the knowledgeable breeder initiates a well-thought-out socialization process.

The governing kennel clubs in the different countries of the world maintain lists of local breed clubs and breeders that can lead a prospective dog buyer to responsible breeders of quality stock. Should you not be sure of where to contact a respected breeder in your area, we strongly recommend contacting your local kennel club for recommendations.

The buyer should look for cleanliness in both the dogs and the areas in which the dogs are kept. Cleanliness is the first clue that tells you how much the breeder cares about the dogs he or she owns.

It is extremely important that the buyer knows the character and quality of a puppy's parents. Good temperament and good health are inherited and if the puppy's parents are not sound in these respects, there is not much likelihood that they will produce offspring that are. Never buy a Doberman from anyone who has no knowledge of the puppy's parents or what kind of care a puppy has been given from birth to the time you see him.

HEALTH CONCERNS

There is every possibility a reputable breeder resides in your area who will not only be able to provide the right Doberman for you but also will have the mother of the puppy on the premises. This gives you an opportunity to see first hand what kind of dogs are in the background of the puppy you are considering. Good breeders are always willing to have you see their dogs and to inspect the facility in which the dogs are raised. These breeders will also be able to discuss problems that exist in the breed with you and how they deal with these problems.

Cardiomyopathy

Cardiomyopathy is progressive deterioration of the heart that eventually results in congestive heart failure and sudden death. Conscientious breeders constantly test to determine the existence of the problem in their line and rigidly cull to eliminate the problem.

Cervical Vertebral Instability

Commonly referred to as "Wobbler Syndrome" or CVI, Cervical Vertebral Instability is a skeletal problem that is most apt to affect dogs four to ten years of age. Its symptoms range from minor lameness to complete paralysis of the hindquarters.

Blue Dobe Syndrome

This is a chronic skin condition that occurs in blue Dobes. It produces a dry, lackluster and moth-eaten coat. Bald patches can develop, but far more consequential is the fact that those Dobermans that are afflicted are highly susceptible to staph infections.

QUESTIONS AND ANSWERS

Describing these diseases that can affect the Doberman is not to indicate that all Doberman lines are afflicted with them. However, the responsible breeder will always be more than happy to discuss his or her experience, if any, with the problems.

A corner of the author's kitchen becomes the perfect nap time spot for her litter of Doberman Pinscher puppies.

All breeds of dogs have genetic problems that must be paid attention to and just because a male and female do not evidence problems, this does not mean their pedigrees are free of something that might be entirely incapacitating. Again, rely upon recommendations from national kennel clubs or local breed clubs when looking for a breeder.

As we have mentioned previously, do not be surprised if a concerned breeder asks many questions about you and the environment in which your Doberman will be raised. Good breeders are just as concerned with the quality of the homes to which their dogs are going as you, the buyer, are with obtaining a sound and healthy dog.

Do not think a good Doberman puppy can only come from a large kennel. On the contrary, today many of the best breeders raise dogs in their homes as a hobby. It is important, however, that you not allow yourself to fall into the hands of an irresponsible "backyard breeder." Backyard breeders separate themselves from the hobby breeder through their total lack of regard for the health of their breeding stock.

They do not test their stock for genetic problems, nor are they concerned with how or where their puppies are raised.

RECOGNIZING A HEALTHY PUPPY

Most Doberman breeders do not release their puppies until the puppies have been given their "puppy shots." Normally, this is at about 7 to 12 weeks of age. At this age they will be weaned from their mother and will bond extremely well with their new owners. Nursing puppies receive temporary immunization from their mother. Once weaned, however, a puppy is highly susceptible to many infectious diseases that can be transmitted via the hands and clothing of people. Therefore, it behooves you to make sure your puppy is fully inoculated before he leaves his home environment and to know when any additional inoculations should be given.

Above all, the Doberman puppy you buy should be a happy, bouncy extrovert. The Doberman's protective instinct develops in adulthood. A shy or suspicious puppy is definitely a poor choice, as is a shy, shrinking-violet puppy or one that appears sick and listless. Selecting a puppy of that sort because you feel sorry for him will undoubtedly lead to heartache and difficulty, to say nothing of the veterinary costs that you may incur in getting the puppy well.

If at all possible, take the puppy you are interested in away from his littermates into another room or another part of the

kennel. The smells will remain the same for the puppy so he should still feel secure and maintain his outgoing personality, but it will give you an opportunity to inspect the puppy more closely. A healthy little Dobe puppy will be strong and sturdy to the

Although a Doberman is capable of braving the coldest of temperatures, Katie, bred by Truslove Kennels, finds snuggling up in a blanket much more appealing.

You can tell a lot about a puppy's personality by observing his interaction with his littermates. This small army of Doberman pups is looking for good homes.

touch, never bony, or on the other hand, obese and bloated. The inside of the puppy's ears should be pink and clean. Dark discharge or a bad odor could indicate ear mites, a sure sign of poor maintenance. The healthy Dobe puppy's breath smells sweet. The teeth are clean and white and there should never be any malformation of the mouth or jaw. The puppy's eyes should be clear, bright, and have a soft, almost wise look. Eyes that appear runny and irritated indicate serious problems.

There should be no sign of discharge from the nose nor should it be crusted or runny. Coughing or diarrhea are danger signals, as are any eruptions on the skin. The coat should be soft and lustrous.

The healthy puppy's front legs should be straight as little posts and strong and true. Of course there is always a chubby, clumsy puppy or two in a litter. Do not mistake this for unsoundness but if ever you have any doubts, discuss them with the breeder.

Male or Female?

While both the male and the female are capable of becoming excellent companions and are equally easy to train, do consider the fact that a male Doberman will be larger, sometimes 20 or 30 pounds heavier than his sister, and he will have all the muscle power to go with the extra weight. Give serious consideration to your own strength and stature.

There are other sex-related differences to consider as well. While the Doberman Pinscher is a clean breed and relatively easy to housebreak, the male provides a problem in that he, like the male of any breed of dog, has a natural instinct to lift his leg and "mark" his territory. The amount of effort that is involved in training the male not to do this varies with the individual dog. What must be remembered is that a male considers everything in the household a part of his territory and has an innate urge to establish this fact. This unfortunately

Socialization with littermates is very important in order to learn how to interact with other dogs. This Dobe puppy tries to give her sister a hand with her new collar.

may include your designer drapery or newly upholstered sofa.

The female of the breed, on the other hand, has her own set of problems. A female has semiannual heat cycles that commence at about one year of age. During these heat cycles of approximately 21 days, the female must be confined to avoid soiling her surroundings with the bloody discharge that accompanies estrus. There are "britches" sold at pet shops that assist in keeping the female in heat from soiling the area in which she lives. She must also be carefully watched to prevent males from gaining access to her or she will become pregnant. The "marauding male" will not be deterred by the britches should your female have them on, so always be on guard!

Spaying or neutering your Doberman will not only help control the pet population, it also lessens the chances of contracting certain diseases later in life.

Both of these sexually related problems can be avoided by having the pet Doberman "altered." Spaying the female and neutering the male saves the pet owner all the headaches of either of the sexually related problems without changing the character of your Doberman. If there is any change at all in the altered Doberman, it is in making the dog an even more amiable companion. Above all, altering your pet precludes the possibility of its adding to the serious pet overpopulation problems that exist worldwide.

SELECTING A SHOW PROSPECT PUPPY

Should you be considering a show career for your puppy, all the foregoing regarding soundness and health apply here as well. Spaying and castration are not reversible procedures and once done they eliminate the possibility of ever breeding or showing your Doberman in conformation shows. Altered dogs can, however, be shown in Obedience Trials and many other competitive events.

There are a good number of additional points to be considered for the show dog. First of all, it should be remembered that the most any breeder can offer is an opinion on the "show potential" of a particular puppy. The most promising eight-week-old Dobe puppy can grow up to be an average adult. A breeder has no control over this.

Any predictions a breeder makes about a puppy's future are based upon his experience with past litters that have produced winning show dogs. It is obvious, the more successful a breeder has been in producing winning Dobermans over the years, the broader his base of comparison will be.

A puppy's potential as a show dog is determined by how closely he adheres to the demands of the standard of the breed.

While most breeders concur there is no such thing as "a sure thing" when it comes to predicting winners, they are also quick to agree that the older a puppy is, the better your chances are of making any predictions. We have found that grading a litter and evaluating the puppies is best done at eight weeks of age.

What a natural! This well-constructed, show prospect Dobe puppy spotted a bird and put himself in a perfect stance.

It makes little difference to the owner of a pet if their Doberman is a bit smaller than the standard or if it has a low tail set. Neither would it make a difference if a male pup had only one testicle. These faults do not interfere with a Doberman becoming a healthy and loving companion, however, they would keep that Doberman from a winning show career.

While it certainly behooves the prospective buyer of a show prospect puppy to be as familiar with the standard of the breed as possible, it is even more important for the buyer to put his or herself into the hands of a successful and respected breeder of winning Dobes. The experienced breeder knows there are certain age-related shortcomings in a young Dobe that maturity will take care of, and there are other faults that completely eliminate the puppy from consideration as a show prospect.

Breeders are always looking for the right homes in which to place their show prospect puppies. They can be particularly helpful if you tell them that you plan to show one of their dogs.

When selecting a dog for show, you must not be swayed by "cuteness" alone. Adorable though he may be, you must seriously consider the puppy's conformation.

The important thing to remember in choosing your first show prospect is that "cuteness" may not be consistent with quality. While showmanship and a charismatic personality are critical to a show dog's success in the ring, those qualities are the frosting on the cake, so to speak. They are the characteristics that put the well-made Doberman over the top.

An extroverted or particularly loving puppy in the litter might decide he belongs to you. If you are simply looking for a pet, that is the puppy for you. However, if you are genuinely interested in showing your Dobe, you must keep your head and, without disregarding good temperament, give serious consideration to what the standard says a show type Doberman Pinscher must be.

Look for the pup in a litter that is sound—both mentally and physically. It must have an outgoing and confident attitude. A

Doberman without a feeling of self-importance will seldom develop into an outstanding show dog. Inherited good temperament and proper socialization are extremely important and it will show throughout the litter, but there are always those "special" Doberman puppies that seem to know they are destined for the show ring.

Any puppy that appears short on his legs or too long in his body should not be considered at all for the show ring. Look for the puppy with the straight, hard topline. The neck should give an arched appearance and it should flow smoothly into the shoulders.

You want a puppy with strong, straight, gun-barrel front legs. A spindly looking pup is all wrong for a Doberman. The feet should be tight and round, what breeders refer to as "cat feet." Flat splayed feet are a serious fault.

The puppy's head should appear to be a wedge, looking at it from above or from the side. There should be a strong underjaw and the teeth should meet in a scissors bite, although a bite in which the upper front teeth extend over the bottom teeth a bit should not create worry. The lower jaw seems to continue growing longer so, more often than not, the slight over-bite will correct itself.

As the standard indicates there are only four allowable Doberman colors: Black, red, blue and fawn. (The fawn color is also known as Isabelle or Isabella.) No other colors may be shown.

All four colors have rust colored markings in specified locations: over each eye, on the throat and chest and on the muzzle. Rust markings are also located under the tail and on the legs. White markings are undesirable.

Tug-of-war with something other than a Nylafloss®— for shame!

There are many nuances of breed type that are best understood by an experienced breeder of show quality Dobermans. Rely upon someone who has had this experience to assist you in selecting a puppy of promise. There is an old breeder's saying that applies well here: "Breed the best to the best. Select the best and then hope for the best!"

If you do not have the time or inclination to train a puppy, a well-trained adult Doberman may be better suited to your lifestyle.

PUPPY OR ADULT?

A young puppy is not your only option when contemplating the purchase of a Doberman, in some cases an adult dog may be just the answer. It certainly eliminates the trials and tribulations of housebreaking, chewing, and the myriad of other problems associated with a young puppy.

On occasion, adult Dobermans are available from homes or kennels breeding show dogs. Their breeders realize the older dog would be far happier in a family situation where he can watch TV, take hikes and be a part of a family instead of living out his life in a kennel run.

Adult Dobermans can adjust to their new homes with relative ease. Most new owners are amazed at how quickly it all happens and how quickly these adults become devoted to their new families! After all, a Doberman lives to have his own person or family and even those raised in a kennel seem to "blossom" in the home environment.

An adult Dobe that has been given kind and loving care in his previous home could be the perfect answer for an elderly person or someone who is forced to be away from home during the day. While it would be unreasonable to expect a young puppy not to relieve himself in the house after you are gone for more than just a few hours, it would be surprising to find an older and housebroken Dobe who would willingly even consider relieving himself in the home in which he lives.

A few adult Dobes may have become set in their ways and while you may not have to contend with the problems of puppyhood, do realize that there is the rare adult that might have developed habits that do not entirely suit you or your lifestyle. Arrange to bring an adult Dobe into your home on a trial basis. That way neither you nor the dog will be obligated should either of you decide you are incompatible.

IDENTIFICATION PAPERS

The purchase of any purebred dog entitles you to three very important documents: a health record containing an inoculation list, a copy of the dog's pedigree, and the registration certificate.

Health Record

Most Dobe breeders have initiated the necessary inoculation series for their puppies by the time they are eight weeks of age. These inoculations protect the puppies against hepatitis, leptospirosis, distemper and canine parvovirus. In most cases rabies inoculations are not given until a puppy is five months of age or older.

There is a set series of inoculations developed to combat these infectious diseases and it is extremely important that you obtain a record of the shots your puppy has been given and the dates upon which the shots were administered. With this record the veterinarian you choose will be able to continue on with the appropriate inoculation series as needed.

Pedigree

The pedigree is your dog's "family tree." The breeder must supply you with a copy of this document authenticating your puppy's ancestors back to at least the third generation. All purebred dogs have a pedigree. The pedigree does not imply that a dog is of show quality, it is simply a chronological list of ancestors.

Registration Certificate

The registration certificate is the canine world's "birth certificate." This certificate is issued by a country's governing kennel club. When you transfer the ownership of your Dobe from the breeder's name to your own name, the transaction is entered on this certificate and once mailed to the kennel club, it is permanently recorded in their computerized files. Keep all these documents in a safe place as you will need them when you visit your veterinarian or should you ever wish to breed or show your Doberman.

DIET SHEET

Your Dobe is the happy healthy puppy he is because the breeder has been carefully feeding and caring for him. Every breeder we know has his own particular way of doing this. Most breeders give the new owner a written record that details the amount and kind of food a puppy has been receiving. Do follow these recommendations to the letter for at least the first month or two after the puppy comes to live with you.

The breeder will have started your Dobe puppy on the road to good nutrition. Dinner time for newly weaned puppies can be a very messy affair!

The diet sheet should indicate the number of times a day your puppy has been accustomed to being fed and the kind of vitamin supplementation (if any) he has been receiving. Following the prescribed procedure will reduce the chance of an upset stomach and loose stools.

Usually a breeder's diet sheet projects the increases and changes in food that will be necessary as your puppy grows from week to week. If the sheet does not include this information, ask the breeder for suggestions regarding increases and the eventual changeover to adult food.

In the unlikely event you are not supplied with a diet sheet by the breeder and are unable to get one, your veterinarian will be able to advise you in this respect. There are countless foods now being manufactured expressly to meet the nutritional needs of puppies and growing dogs. A trip down the pet aisle at your supermarket or pet supply store will prove just how many choices you have. Two important tips to remember: read labels carefully for content and when dealing with established, reliable manufacturers, you are more likely to get what you pay for.

If you properly socialize your Doberman when he is young, he will be able to make friends easily. This HoMike teenager enjoys a tug-of-war with his Cocker Spaniel buddy.

Health Guarantee

Any reputable breeder will be more than willing to supply a written agreement that the sale of your Dobe is contingent upon his

Bonding with love and affection—that is what dog ownership is all about.

passing a veterinarian's examination. Ideally you will be able to arrange an appointment with your chosen veterinarian right after you have picked up your puppy from the breeder and before you take the puppy home. If this is not possible, you should not delay this procedure any longer than 24 hours from the time you take your puppy home.

TEMPERAMENT AND SOCIALIZATION

Temperament is both hereditary and learned. Inherited good temperament can be ruined by poor treatment and lack of proper socialization. A Doberman puppy that has inherited bad temperament is a poor risk as a companion or as a show dog and should certainly never be bred. It is critical that you obtain a happy puppy from a breeder who is determined to produce good temperaments and who has taken all the necessary steps to provide the necessary early socialization.

As long as they are properly introduced and closely supervised, your Doberman puppy should get along famously with other pets.

Temperaments in the same litter can range from strong-willed and outgoing on the high end of the scale to reserved and retiring at the low end. A puppy that is so bold and strong-willed as to be foolhardy and uncontrollable could easily be a difficult adult that needs a very firm hand. In a breed as large and strong as a Doberman, this would hardly be a dog for the owner who is mild and reserved in demeanor or frail in physique. In every human–canine relationship there must be a pack leader and a follower. In order to achieve his full potential, the Doberman must have an owner who remains in charge at all times. The Doberman himself wants and needs this kind of relationship.

It is important to remember a Doberman puppy may be as happy as a clam living at home with you and your family but if the socialization begun by the breeder is not continued, that sunny disposition will not extend outside your front door. From the day the young Dobe arrives at your home you must be committed to accompanying him upon an unending pilgrimage to meet and coexist with all human beings and animals. Do not worry about the Doberman's protective instinct. This comes with maturity. Aggressive behavior from your puppy should never be encouraged, and there should not be any reason for the puppy to fear strangers.

If you are fortunate enough to have young children in the household or living nearby, your socialization task will be assisted considerably. Dobermans raised with children seem to have a distinct advantage in socialization. Children must be supervised at all times with the puppy so that they understand how the puppy must be treated.

Brookmeadow's Family Edition, or Duke as he is known to his friends, immediately adopts his owner's grandchild–showing the sweet and protective side of the breed.

Dobermans are apt to "adopt" the household's children and make raising them their own special project. Children and Dobe puppies seem to understand each other and in some way, known only to the puppies and children themselves, they give each other the confidence to face the trying ordeal of growing up.

The children in your own household are not the only children your puppy should spend time with. It is a case of the more the merrier! Every child (and adult for that matter) that enters your household should be asked to pet your puppy.

Your puppy should go everywhere with you: the post office, the market, to the shopping mall, etc. Be prepared to create a stir wherever you go. The public seems to hold a special admiration for the Doberman and while they might not want to approach a mature dog, most people are quite taken with the Dobe puppy and will undoubtedly want to pet your youngster. There is nothing in the world better for the puppy!

Should your puppy back off from a stranger, give the person a treat to offer your puppy. You must insist your young Dobe be amenable to the attention of any strangers you approve of, regardless of sex, age or race. It is not up to your puppy to decide who he will or will not tolerate. You are in charge. You must call the shots.

If your Dobe has a show career in his future, there are other things in addition to just being handled that he will have to learn. All show dogs must learn to have their mouths opened and inspected by the judge. The judge must be able to check the teeth. Males must be accustomed to having their testicles touched as the dog show judge must determine that all male dogs are "complete." This means there are two normal sized testicles in the scrotum. These inspections must begin in puppyhood and be done on a regular and continuing basis.

Four-month-old Truslove's Brka Javkovic is an example of a Doberman with a natural earset.

All Dobermans must learn to get along with other dogs as well as with humans. If you are fortunate enough to have a "puppy preschool" or dog training class nearby, attend with as much regularity as you possibly can. A young Dobe that has been exposed regularly to other dogs from puppyhood will learn to adapt and accept other dogs and other breeds much more readily than one that seldom ever sees strange dogs.

EAR AND TAIL CROPPING

Undoubtedly the Doberman puppy you buy will have had his tail docked and the dewclaws removed. The dewclaws are the additional claws that grow just above the inside part of the foot. This usually takes place within a few days after the puppy is born, before the central nervous system is fully developed.

The decision to crop your Doberman's ears is a personal one. Melissa Kingley lavishes extra care on her little "conehead."

Accomplished at this early age, there is no pain to speak of and little bleeding takes place. There seems to be no apparent reason for the dewclaws at this stage of canine development and active dogs frequently sustain injuries to these superfluous appendages, often ripping them entirely off causing great pain. For this reason, the claws are removed easily and painlessly just after birth.

Those who raise or who have previously owned Doberman Pinschers know what an enthusiastic breed he is. A Dobe registers enthusiasm with his tail, and the

At three months of age, this Doberman's ears are standing correctly.

longer the tail, the more destructive the results can be! An undocked Doberman tail can cause havoc in the household, quickly clearing tables and upending little children. Also, since it is the last part of the Dobe's anatomy exiting a room, it is not unusual for that tail to become injured or broken by a closing door. Those of us who have owned Dobermans are certain the breed is far better off with his tail docked.

Today, ear cropping is deemed to be cosmetic and, if nothing else, customary. The originators of the breed felt it protected the Dobermans from being grasped by the clenches of an adversary. Today's fanciers believe it gives the breed a more elegant look. There is little doubt the latter is true, but ear cropping is a matter of choice on the part of the owner.

Should the decision be made that the cropped ear looks best, the operation should never be performed by anyone other than a veterinarian and that veterinarian should be expert at cropping Doberman Pinscher ears. Ear crops differ from breed to breed and you will want to be sure the style is suitable for your Doberman. The breeder from whom you purchase your Dobe puppy will undoubtedly be able to make recommendations as to where you might have your dog's ears cropped. This is very important in that in addition to the actual cropping there is a system of care that follows the procedure best prescribed by the individual that does the cropping.

THE ADOLESCENT DOBERMAN PINSCHER

You will find it amazing how quickly the tiny youngster you first

Although today ear cropping is done primarily for looks, its original intent was a practical one—it protected the Doberman from being grabbed by an adversary.

brought home begins to develop into a full grown Doberman Pinscher. Some lines shoot up to full size very rapidly, others mature more slowly. At about five months, most Doberman puppies become lanky and ungainly, growing in and out of proportion seemingly from one day to the next.

Somewhere around 12 months your Dobe will have attained his full height. Body and muscle development continue on, however, until two years of age in some lines and up to three and almost four in others.

Food needs increase during this growth period and the average Doberman seems as if he can never get enough to eat. There are some that experience a very finicky stage in their eating habits and seem to eat just enough to keep from starving. Think of Doberman puppies as individual as children and act accordingly.

The amount of food you give your Doberman should be adjusted to how much he will readily consume at each meal. If the entire meal is eaten quickly, add a small amount to the next feeding and continue to do so as the need

Your little Doberman puppy will soon be a very large adult, so he must learn to conform to the rules of the household. This guy has to give up his job as "laundry thief."

A puppy is filled with curiosity and endless energy. Be sure to carefully supervise your Dobe to keep him out of mischief.

increases. This method will ensure you give your puppy enough food but you must also pay close attention to the dog's appearance and condition, as you do not want a puppy to become overweight or obese.

At eight weeks of age, a Dobe puppy is eating four meals a day. By the time he is six months old, the puppy can do well on two meals a day with perhaps a snack in the middle of the day. If your puppy does not eat the food offered, he is either not hungry or not well. Your Dobe will eat when he is hungry. If you suspect the dog is not well, a trip to the veterinarian is in order.

This adolescent period is a particularly important one as it is the time your Dobe must learn all the household and social rules by which he will live for the rest of his life. Your patience and commitment during this time will not only produce an obedient canine, but will forge a bond between the two of you that will grow and ripen into a wonderful relationship.

CARING for Your Doberman Pinscher

FEEDING AND NUTRITION

Following the diet sheet provided by the breeder from whom you purchase your puppy is the best way to make sure your Doberman is obtaining the right amount and the correct type of food for his age. Do your best not to change the puppy's diet and you will be far less apt to run into digestive problems and diarrhea. Diarrhea is something that is very serious in young puppies. Puppies with diarrhea can dehydrate very rapidly causing severe problems and even death.

If it is necessary to change your puppy's diet for any reason, it should never be done abruptly. Begin by adding a tablespoon or two of the new food and reduce the old product by the same amount. Gradually increase the amount of the new food over a week or ten days until the meal consists entirely of the new product. A puppy's digestive system is extremely delicate. Any changes you make in what he eats should be done carefully and slowly.

The amount of food you give your Dobe puppy should also be adjusted carefully. Give the puppy all he will eat within 10 or 15 minutes of the time you put the food dish down. Take the dish up after that amount of time has elapsed. If the puppy consumes the entire meal, add a small amount to the next meal, balancing what you add with what the puppy will eat.

Your breeder will have started your puppy on a healthy diet, so stick to it and make any changes gradual.

There is the occasional Dobe puppy that is a true glutton and he will eat more than he needs to stay healthy. A good rule of thumb is this: you should be able to feel the ribs and backbone with just a slight layer of fat

Feed your Doberman a good-quality dog food so he gets the nutrients he needs.

Very young pups get all the nutrients they need through nursing. As they grow, you, the owner, will be responsible for providing a well-balanced diet.

and muscle over them. The puppy should be firm to the touch and not sloppy with rolls of loose flesh.

By the time your Dobe puppy is 12 months old you can reduce feedings to two a day. There are two important things to remember: feed the main meal at the same time every day and make sure what you feed is nutritionally complete.

Make sure your Doberman has cool, clean water available at all times, especially after exercising outside.

Never feed your dog within 90 minutes of any type of strenuous activity. Doing so could cause bloat, a rotation of the stomach that closes off both ends. This condition is extremely painful and often fatal. Excessive amounts of water to cool your dog quickly if he is overheated is also dangerous. Wait until the dog has cooled down.

A morning or nighttime snack of hard dog biscuits made especially for large dogs can also be given in addition to the diet. These biscuits become highly anticipated treats by your Dobe.

"Balanced" Diets

In the US, dog foods must meet standards set by the Subcommittee on Canine Nutrition of the National Research Council in order to qualify as "complete and balanced." As proof of compliance, dog food manufacturers list the ingredients of their product on every box, bag, or can. The ingredients are listed by weight in descending order.

Do not feed your Doberman sugar products and avoid products which contain sugar to any high degree. Excessive amounts of these sugars can lead to severe dental problems and unwanted weight gain.

To achieve optimum health and condition make sure your Doberman has a constant supply of fresh clean water and a balanced diet containing the essential nutrients in correct proportions. This can be achieved with a good quality kibble to which a small amount of canned, fresh or cooked meat can be added. Pet stores and supermarkets all carry a wide selection of foods manufactured by respected firms. An important thing to remember in selecting these foods is that all dogs are meat-eating animals. Animal protein and fats are absolutely essential to the well being of any breed of dog.

The main ingredient in any commercially prepared food you buy should be animal protein. The remaining ingredients in

quality products will provide the carbohydrates, fats, roughage, and correct amounts of minerals your dog needs.

Some dry foods may not contain the amount of fat that will keep the Doberman's coat in top condition. If your dog's coat appears dry and seems to lack luster, a very small amount of animal fat such as bacon drippings, beef trimmings or peanut or canola oil can be beneficially added to the diet, particularly during winter weather.

Over-Supplementation

A great deal of controversy exists today regarding the orthopedic problems in dogs, specifically, hip, elbow, and patella (knee) dysplasia. Some claim these problems and a wide variety of chronic skin conditions are entirely hereditary. Others feel they are a result, in whole or in part, of overuse of mineral and vitamin supplements in puppies and young dogs.

When vitamins are used, the prescribed amount should never be exceeded. Some breeders insist all recommended dosages be cut in half when used with the heavily fortified commercial foods.

There may be special periods in a Dobe's life when vitamin supplementation is necessary. The time of rapid growth the breed experiences in puppyhood, the female's pregnancy and the time during which she is nursing her puppies are high stress periods and your veterinarian may suggest vitamin supplementation.

Never feed your Dobe from the table while you are eating. Dogs can quickly become addicted to the "exotic" smells of the foods you eat and turn up their nose at the less tempting, but probably far more nutritious, food in his regular meals.

Dogs do not care if food looks like a hot dog or wedge of cheese. They only care about the food's smell and its taste. Products manufactured to "look like" other foods are designed to appeal to the humans who buy them. These foods often contain high amounts of preservatives, sugars and dyes none of which are suitable for your dog.

Special Diets

Commercially prepared diets are available for dogs with special dietary needs. The overweight, underweight, or geriatric dog can have his nutritional needs met, as can puppies and growing dogs. The calorie content of these foods is adjusted accordingly.

Common sense must prevail. What works for humans works for dogs as well—too many calories and too little exercise will increase weight, stepping up exercise and reducing the calorie count will bring weight down.

Occasionally an adolescent Dobe will become a problem eater. Trying to tempt the dog to eat by hand-feeding or offering special foods only serves to make the problem worse. Your dog will quickly learn to play the waiting game, fully aware that those special things he likes will arrive—probably sooner than later. Feed your Doberman the proper food you want him to eat. The dog may turn up his nose for a day or two and refuse to eat anything, but you can rest assured when your dog is really hungry, he will eat.

Bathe your Doberman only when absolutely necessary. This Dobe is enjoying a bubble bath!

Unlike humans, dogs have no suicidal tendencies. A healthy dog will not starve himself to death. He may not eat enough to keep himself in the shape we find ideal and attractive, but he will definitely eat enough to maintain himself. If your Dobe is not eating properly and appears to be thin and listless, it is probably best to consult your veterinarian.

BATHING AND GROOMING

Your Dobe will not require much of your time or equipment in the way of grooming but that is not to say that he needs no care at all in this respect. Regular brushing keeps the coat clean, odor-free, and healthy. Wiping the coat off with a solution of warm water to which is added one capful each of bleach and a mild bath oil will act as an excellent coat conditioner and help to kill any fungus that may have taken hold.

Regular grooming gives you the opportunity to keep on top of your dog's home health care needs. If you find your dog is licking himself and causing an irritation, try applying a foul-tasting but non-toxic liquid that will not harm the dog in any way, available at most pet stores. Use an antiseptic on any scratches you should find.

Such things as trimming nails, cleaning ears, and checking teeth can be attended to at this time as well. Investing in a grooming table that has a non-slip top and an arm and noose can make all of these activities much easier. These tables are available at pet shops.

Undoubtedly, the breeder from whom you purchased your

Dobe will have begun to accustom the puppy to grooming just as soon as he was old enough to stand. You must continue on with grooming sessions or begin them at once if for some reason they have not been started. It is imperative you both learn to cooperate in this endeavor in order to make it an easy and pleasant experience.

Your Doberman Pinscher should become accustomed to grooming procedures, like nail trimming, at an early age.

Brush with the lay of the hair using a brush or a glove with short rubber nubs. A fine spray of coat dressing and a quick rub with a towel or wash cloth will give your Dobe's coat a real glow.

Your Doberman should be accustomed to having his nails trimmed and his feet inspected. Always inspect your dog's feet for cracked pads. Check between the toes for splinters and thorns, and pay particular attention to any swollen or tender areas.

We suggest attending to your dog's nails at least every other week. Long nails on a Doberman are not only unattractive, but they spread and weaken the foot. The nails of a Dobe that doesn't exercise outdoors on rough terrain will grow long very quickly. Do not allow the nails to become overgrown and then expect to cut them back easily. Each nail has a blood vessel running through the center called the "quick." The quick

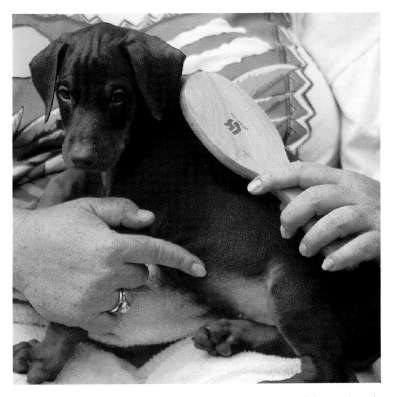

Regular brushing will keep your Doberman's coat clean, shiny and odor free.

grows close to the end of the nail and contains very sensitive nerve endings. If the nail is allowed to grow too long, it will be impossible to cut it back to a proper length without cutting into the quick. This causes severe pain to the dog and can also result in a great deal of bleeding that can be very difficult to stop.

Nails can be trimmed with canine nail clippers or an electric nail grinder. We prefer the latter using a "fine" grinding disc because this allows you to trim back the nail a little bit at a time. The Dobe's dark nails make it practically impossible to see where the quick ends, so regardless of which nail trimming device is used, you must proceed with caution and remove only a small portion of the nail at a time.

Should the quick be nipped in the trimming process, there are a number of blood-clotting products available at pet shops that will almost immediately stop the flow of blood. It is wise to have one of these products on hand in case the quick is clipped. Dobermans look much better with their whiskers trimmed. This can be done with a good pair of blunt tip barber sheers. The rounded tips preclude the possibility of your Dobe injuring his eye by making a sudden move.

Regular brushing practically eliminates the need for giving your Doberman a wet bath. If your dog finds his way into some foul-smelling substance, there are many "dry bath" products that can be used that both clean the coat and eliminate odor.

Care should always be given to the state of your dog's teeth. If your dog has been accustomed to chewing hard dog biscuits or gnawing on large rawhide bones or any of the wide variety of Nylabone® products since puppyhood, it is unlikely that you will have any dental problems. This chewing activity assists greatly in removing dental plaque, which is the major cause of tooth decay. Any sign of redness of the gums or tooth decay merits expert attention.

EXERCISE

The Dobe that is given plenty of opportunity to exercise is a much happier and healthier dog. Any dog that expends his energy in physical activity is far less apt to become mischievous and destructive in the home.

Needless to say, puppies should never be forced to exercise. Normally, they are little dynamos of energy and keep themselves busy all day long but intersperse playtime with frequent naps.

As far as the adult Doberman is concerned, he can do pretty much all of the things his owner can do in the line of exercise:

Socialization should continue throughout your Doberman's life. The more people and pets he meets, the better.

walk, jog, hike, swim, and play all kinds of games. This can do nothing but benefit the Dobe, to say nothing of the dog's owner!

Mature Dobes are capable and enthusiastic jogging companions. They can also be exercised using a bicycle attachment made specifically for

A healthy Doberman Pinscher can participate in almost any athletic endeavor. This Doberman goes for a dip in the ocean.

dogs. It is important, however, to use good judgment in any exercise program. Begin slowly and increase the distance to be covered very gradually over an extended period of time. Use special precautions in hot weather. High temperatures and forced exercise are a dangerous combination.

SOCIALIZATION

A young Dobe that has never been exposed to strangers, traffic noises, or boisterous children could become confused and frightened. It is important that a Dobe owner give his or her dog the opportunity to experience all of these situations gradually, with his trusted owner present for support.

Doberman puppies are usually friendly and more than happy to accept strangers but as they mature, their attitudes can change. They can become reserved and suspicious if the socialization process is neglected. It is absolutely imperative that you continue the socialization process and maintain the pack leader role with your Doberman as he matures.

A well-trained Doberman can serve both as a guard dog and as a good citizen. The dog knows he must obey your commands under all circumstances, that "no!" means just that, and once you give that command, he must stop whatever he is doing.

TRAINING Your Doberman Pinscher

There is no breed of dog that cannot be trained. Granted, there are some dogs that provide a real challenge to this concept, but in most cases this has more to do with the trainer and his or her training methods than with the dog's inability to learn. Using the proper approach, any dog that is not mentally deficient can be taught to be a good canine citizen. Many dog owners do not understand how a dog learns nor do they realize they can be breed specific in their approach to training.

A Doberman Pinscher is as smart as his owner allows him to be. The Doberman owner is extremely fortunate in that the breed is not only highly capable of learning, he thrives on training.

Young Doberman puppies have an amazing capacity to learn. This capacity is greater than most humans realize. It is important to remember though, that these young puppies also forget with great speed unless they are reminded of what they have learned by continual reinforcement.

As puppies leave the nest they begin their search for two things: a pack leader and the rules set down by that leader by which the puppies can abide. Dog owners often fail miserably in supplying these very basic needs. Instead, the owner immediately begins to respond to the demands of the puppy and puppies can quickly learn to be very demanding. In the case of little dogs this can be a nuisance.

In the case of large dogs, like the Doberman, this can produce an aggressive and uncontrollable danger to society.

A well-trained Doberman is a joy to own. This pair of Ryansluxus Dobermans have been trained to do their owners a real service!

If you allow your Dobe puppy to develop bad habits, like sleeping on the bed, it will be harder to break him of them later on.

A puppy quickly learns that misbehavior gets attention. He will learn that he will be allowed into the house because he is whining, not because he can only enter the house when he is not whining. For the puppy to learn the only way, he must follow a set procedure every time it is to enter (i.e., sitting or lying down on command) and then be permitted in. The poorly educated Dobe puppy learns that leaping about, whining, and creating a stir is what gets results, and this must be corrected to obedient behavior is what gets results.

If your Doberman finds that a growl or a snap can permit him to have his own way, rest assured that behavior will continue. In fact, the behavior will only increase. On the other hand, if a challenge on the part of the dog is met with stern, uncompromising correction, the dog knows that behavior such as this does not evoke the desired response.

If the young puppy cannot find his pack leader in his owner, the puppy assumes the role of pack leader. If there are no rules imposed, the puppy learns to make his own rules.

Unfortunately the negligent owner continually reinforces the puppy's decisions by allowing him to govern the household.

The key to successful training lies in establishing the proper relationship between dog and owner. The owner or the owning family must be the pack leader and the individual or family must provide the rules by which the dog is to abide.

The Doberman is

Allocate an area of your home, such as the kitchen, to your Doberman puppy until he is housebroken.

easily trained to almost any task. It is important to remember, however, that the breed does not comprehend violent treatment nor does the Doberman need it. Positive reinforcement is the key to successfully training a Doberman Pinscher and it produces a happy, confident companion.

A Dobe puppy should always be a winner. Begin teaching simple lessons like the "come" command when the puppy is already on his way to you. Do not expect the young puppy to come dashing over to you when he is engrossed in some wonderful adventure. The puppy quickly learns he will be praised for coming on command rather than associating the word with anger on the part of its owner because he did not respond to the word "come."

HOUSEBREAKING MADE EASY

The best method of housebreaking your Doberman puppy is to avoid an accident happening in the first place. Our motto is, "Puppies don't make mistakes, people do." The young puppy has no idea what housebreaking means, therefore he can hardly be accused of breaking a rule! You must teach the puppy what a fine little tyke he is by attending to his toilet needs outdoors or on paper.

Good nutrition will be evident in your dog's healthy appearance and enthusiastic attitude.

Take a puppy outdoors to relieve himself after every meal, after every nap, and after every 15 or 20 minutes of playtime. Carry the puppy outdoors to avoid the opportunity of an accident occurring on the way.

Housebreaking is a much easier task with the use of a crate. Most breeders use the fiberglass-type crates approved by the airlines for shipping live animals. They are easy to clean and can be used for the entire life of the dog.

Some first-time dog owners may see the crate method of housebreaking as cruel. What they do not understand is that all dogs need a place of their own to retreat to. A puppy will soon look to his crate as his own private den.

The use of a crate reduces housetraining time down to an absolute minimum and avoids keeping a puppy under constant stress by incessantly correcting him for making mistakes in the house. The anti-crate advocates who consider it cruel to confine a puppy for any length of time do not seem to have a

problem with constantly harassing and punishing the puppy because he has wet on the carpet and relieved himself behind the sofa.

Crate training begins with feeding your puppy while in the crate. Keep the door closed and latched while the puppy is eating. When the meal is finished, open the crate and carry the puppy outdoors to the spot where you want him to learn to eliminate. In the event you do not have outdoor access or will be away from home for long periods of time, begin housebreaking by placing newspapers in some out of the way corner that is easily accessible for the puppy. If you consistently take your puppy to the same spot you will reinforce the habit of going there for that purpose.

Begin housebreaking your Dobe puppy by placing newspapers on the floor and eventually moving the paper closer and closer to the door.

It is important that you do not let the puppy loose after eating. Young puppies will eliminate almost immediately after eating or drinking. They will also be ready to relieve themselves when they first wake up and after playing. If you keep a watchful eye on your puppy you will quickly learn when this is about to take place. A puppy usually circles and sniffs the floor just before he will relieve himself.

Do not give your puppy an opportunity to learn that he can eliminate in the house! Should an accident occur you must correct the puppy when he is in the act of relieving himself. A puppy does not understand what you are talking about when you reprimand him for something he did even minutes before. Reprimand at the time of the act or not at all. Your house-training chores will be reduced considerably if you avoid bad habits beginning in the first place.

If you are not able to watch your puppy every minute, he should be in his crate with the door securely latched. Each time you put your puppy in the crate, give him a small treat of some kind. Throw the treat to the back of the crate and encourage the puppy to walk in on his own. When he does so, praise the puppy and perhaps hand him

Your Doberman Pinscher will come to think of his crate as his cozy retreat— a home away from home.

71

another piece of the treat through the wires of the cage.

Understand that a Doberman puppy of 8 to 12 weeks will not be able to contain himself for long periods of time. Puppies of that age must relieve themselves often except at night. Never leave a very young puppy in a crate for more than four hours during the day. Your schedule must be adjusted accordingly. Also make sure your puppy has relieved himself at night before the last member of the family retires.

Your first priority in the morning is to get the puppy outdoors. Just how early this will take place will depend much more upon your puppy than upon you. If your Dobe puppy is like most others, there will be no doubt in your mind when he needs to be let out. You will also very quickly learn to tell the difference between the puppy's "emergency" signals and just unhappy grumbling. Do not test the young puppy's ability to contain himself. His vocal demand to be let out is confirmation that the housebreaking lesson is being learned.

You must train your Doberman to walk on a leash for his safety, as well as the safety of others.

Should you find it necessary to be away from home all day, you will not be able to leave your puppy in a crate; however, do not make the mistake of allowing him to roam the house or even a large room at will.

Confine the puppy to a small room or a partitioned-off area and cover the floor with newspaper. Make this area large enough so that the puppy will not have to relieve himself next to his bed, food or water bowls. You will soon find the puppy will be inclined to use one particular spot to perform his bowel and bladder functions. When you are home you must take the puppy to this exact spot to eliminate at the appropriate time.

BASIC TRAINING

The Doberman is a ready, willing, and eager student. As previously stated, the breed thrives on learning. Make sure you, too, are in the right frame of mind for training sessions. Training should never take place when you are irritated, distressed or preoccupied. Nor should you begin basic training in crowded or noisy places that will

Teach your Doberman to be gentle around children and never leave a child and a dog unsupervised.

interfere with you or your dog's concentration. Once the commands are understood and learned you can begin testing your dog in public places, but at first the two of you should work in a place where you can fully concentrate upon each other.

The "No!" Command

The most important command your Dobe puppy will ever learn is the meaning of "no!" This is the command the puppy can begin learning the minute he first arrives in your home. It is not necessary to frighten the puppy into learning the meaning of the "no" command, but it is critical that you never give this or any other command you are not prepared and able to enforce! The only way a puppy learns to obey commands is to realize that once issued, commands must be obeyed. Always show the pup the correct behavior after the no command.

Leash Training

It is never too early to accustom your Dobe puppy to his leash and collar. The leash and collar are your fail-safe way of keeping your dog under control. It may not be necessary for the puppy or adult Dobe to wear his collar and identification tags within the confines of your home, but no dog should ever leave home without a collar and without the leash held securely in your hand.

It is best to begin getting your puppy accustomed to his collar by leaving a soft collar around his neck for a few minutes at a time. Gradually extend the time you leave the collar on. Most Dobe puppies become accustomed to their collar very quickly and after a few scratches to remove it, they forget they are even wearing one.

While you are playing with the puppy, attach a lightweight leash to the collar. Do not try to guide the puppy at first. The point here is to accustom the puppy to the feeling of having something attached to the collar.

Encourage your puppy to follow you as you move away. Should the puppy be reluctant to cooperate, coax him along with a treat of some kind. Hold the treat in front of the puppy's nose to encourage him to follow you. Just as soon as the puppy takes a few steps toward you, praise him enthusiastically and continue to do so as you continue to move along.

Make the initial sessions short and fun. Continue the lessons in your home or yard until the puppy is completely unconcerned about the fact that he is on a leash. With a treat in one hand and the leash in the other, you can begin to use both to guide the puppy in the direction you wish to go. Begin your first walks in front of the house and eventually extend them down the street and around the block.

The "Come" Command

The next most important lesson for the Dobe puppy to learn is to come when called. It is for this reason that it is very important the puppy learn his name as soon as possible. Constantly repeating the dog's name is what does the trick. Use the puppy's name every time you speak to it. "Want to go outside, Rex?"

"Come Rex, come!"

Learning to "come" on command could save your Dobe's life when the two of you venture out into the world. "Come" is the command a dog must obey without question, but the dog should not associate that command with fear. Your dog's response to his name and the word "come" should always be associated with a pleasant experience such as great praise and petting or a food treat.

All too often, novice trainers get very angry at their dog for not responding immediately to the "come" command. When the dog finally does come, the owner scolds the dog for not obeying. The dog begins to associate "come" with an unpleasant result.

It is much easier to avoid the establishment of bad habits than it is to correct them once set. Avoid at all costs giving the "come" command unless you are sure your puppy will come to you. The very young puppy is far more inclined to respond to learning the "come" command than the older dog. Use the command initially when the puppy is already on his way to you or give the command while walking or running away from the youngster. Clap your hands and sound very happy and excited about having the puppy join in on this "game."

The come command is easy to teach a young puppy because he usually wants to be around his owners.

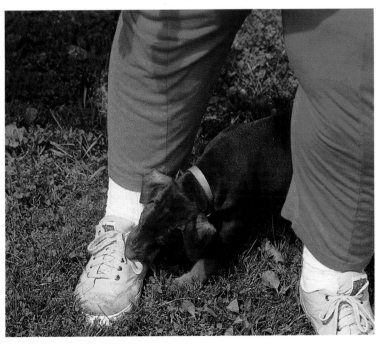

The very young Dobe will normally want to stay as close to his owner as possible, especially in strange surroundings. When your puppy sees you moving away, his natural inclination will be to get close to you. This is a perfect time to use the "come" command.

Later, as a puppy grows more self confident and independent, you may want to attach a long leash or rope to the puppy's collar to ensure the correct response. Again, do not chase or punish your puppy for not obeying the "come" command. Doing so in the initial stages of training makes the youngster associate the command with something to fear and this will result in avoidance rather than the immediate positive response you desire. It is imperative that you praise your puppy and give him a treat when he does come to you, even if he voluntarily delays responding for many minutes.

THE "SIT" AND "STAY" COMMANDS

Just as important to your Dobe's safety (and your sanity!) as the "no!" command and learning to come when called are the "sit" and "stay" commands. Many Dobe puppies learn the sit command easily, especially if it appears to be a game and a food treat is involved.

Your puppy should always be on collar and leash for his lessons. A young puppy is not beyond getting up and walking away when he has decided you and your lessons are boring.

Give the "sit" command immediately before pushing down on your puppy's hindquarters or scooping his hind legs under the dog, molding him into a sit position. Praise the puppy lavishly when he does sit, even though it is you who made the action take place. Again, a food treat always seems to get the lesson across to the learning youngster.

Continue holding the dog's rear end down and repeat the "sit" command several times. If your dog makes an attempt to get up, repeat the command yet again, while exerting pressure on the rear end until the correct position is assumed. Make your Dobe stay in this position for increasing lengths of time. Begin with a few seconds and increase the time as lessons progress over the following weeks.

Should your young student attempt to get up or to lie down, he should be corrected by simply saying, "sit!" in a firm voice. This should be accompanied by returning the dog to the desired position. Only when you decide your dog should get up should he be allowed to do so.

Do not test a very young puppy's patience to the limits. As brilliant as the Doberman Pinscher is, remember you are dealing with a baby. The attention span of any youngster, canine or human, is relatively short.

When you do decide your puppy can get up, call his name, say "OK" and make a big fuss over him. Praise and a food treat are in order every time your puppy responds correctly. Continue to help your puppy assume proper positions or respond to commands until he performs on his own. This way the puppy always wins—he gets it right every time. You are training with positive reinforcement.

This Doberman pup uses his "sit" to pose for a pretty picture!

Once your puppy has mastered the "sit" lesson you may start on the "stay" command. With your dog on leash and facing you, command him to "sit," then take a step or two back. If your dog attempts to get up to follow, firmly say, "sit, stay!" While you are saying this raise your hand, palm toward the dog, and again command "stay!"

Any attempt on your dog's part to get up must be corrected at once, returning him to the sit position and repeating, "stay!" Once your Dobe begins to understand what you want, you can gradually increase the distance you step back. With a long leash attached to your dog's collar (even a clothesline will do) start with a few steps and gradually increase the distance to several yards. Your Dobe must eventually learn the "sit, stay" command must be obeyed no matter how far away you are. Later on, with advanced training, your dog will learn the command is to be obeyed even when you move entirely out of sight.

As your Dobe masters this lesson and is able to remain in the sit position for as long as you dictate, avoid calling your dog to you. This makes the dog overly anxious to get up and run to you. Instead, walk back to your dog and say "OK," a signal that the command is over. Later, when your Dobe becomes more reliable in this respect, you can call him to you.

It is best to keep the "stay" part of the lesson to a minimum until the puppy is at least five or six months old. Everything in a very young Dobe's makeup urges him to stay close to you wherever you go. The puppy has bonded to you and forcing him to operate against his natural instincts can be bewildering.

Praise and affection are the best training motivators for your Doberman Pinscher.

The "Down" Command

Once your Dobe has mastered the "sit" and "stay" commands, you may begin work on "down." This is the single word command for lie down. Use the "down" command only when you want the dog to lie down. If you want your dog to get off your sofa or to stop jumping up on people use the "off" command. Do not interchange these two commands. Doing so will only serve to confuse your dog and evoking the right response will become next to impossible.

The "down" position is especially useful if you want your Doberman to remain in a particular place for a long period of time. A dog is usually far more inclined to stay put when he is lying down than when he is sitting.

Teaching this command to your Dobe may take a little more time and patience than the previous lessons. It is believed by some animal behaviorists that assuming the "down" position somehow represents submissiveness to the dog.

With your Dobe sitting in front of and facing you, hold a treat in your right hand and the excess part of the leash in your left hand. Hold the treat under the dog's nose and slowly bring your hand down to the ground. Your dog will follow the treat with his head and neck. As he does, give the command "down" and exert light pressure on the dog's shoulders with your left hand. If your dog resists the pressure on his shoulders, do not continue pushing down, doing so will only create more resistance.

An alternative method of getting your Dobe headed into the down position is to move around to the dog's right side and as

you draw his attention downward with your right hand, slide your left arm under the dog's front legs and gently slide them forward. In the case of a small puppy, you will undoubtedly have to be on your knees next to the youngster.

As your Dobe's forelegs begin to slide out to his front, keep moving the treat along the ground until the dog's whole body is lying on the ground while you continually repeat "down." Once your Dobe has assumed the position you desire, give him the treat and a lot of praise. Continue assisting your dog into the "down" position until he does so on his own. Be firm and be patient.

The "Heel" Command

In learning to heel, your Doberman will walk on your left side with his shoulder next to your leg no matter which direction you might go or how quickly you turn. *Glen Eagle's Ace Of Spades, CGC, owned by Roslyn Jenkins, practices the heel.*

A training class is the ideal place for socialization and to begin more advanced training for your Doberman. These Ryansluxus Dobermans are at obedience class with their owners.

It is also very important for your dog to understand this command when the two of you are out walking. Teaching your Doberman to heel will not only make your daily walks far more enjoyable, it will make a far more tractable companion when the two of you are in crowded or confusing situations.

Understand that many uninformed people are frightened when they see a Doberman coming down the street. A Doberman lunging at the end of the leash, even if it is done to greet the passer-by, can be extremely intimidating, and the heel command will be comforting to the stranger.

We have found that a lightweight, link-chain training collar is very useful for the heeling lesson. It provides both quick pressure around the neck and a snapping sound, both of which get the dog's attention. Erroneously referred to as a "choke collar," the link-chain collar used properly does not choke the dog. The pet shop at which you purchase the training collar will be able to show you the proper way to put this collar on your dog. Do not leave this collar on your puppy when training sessions are finished. Since the collars fit loosely, they can get hooked and cause injury or even death.

As you train your puppy to walk along on the leash, you should accustom the youngster to walk on your left side. The leash should cross your body from the dog's collar to your right hand. The excess portion of the leash will be folded into your right hand and your left hand on the leash will be used to make corrections with the leash.

Be sure to reward your Doberman pup when he does well and end each session with some quality play time.

A quick, short jerk on the leash with your left hand will keep your dog from lunging side to side, pulling ahead or lagging back. As you make a correction, give the "heel" command. Keep the leash slack as long as your dog maintains the proper position at your side.

If your dog begins to drift away, give the leash a sharp jerk and guide the dog back to the correct position and give the "heel" command. Do not pull on the lead with steady pressure. What is needed is a sharp but gentle jerking motion to get your dog's attention.

TRAINING CLASSES

As we mentioned before, the Doberman is only limited in his education by his owner. There are few limits to what a patient, consistent owner can teach his or her Dobe. For advanced obedience work beyond the basics, it is wise for the Doberman owner to consider local professional assistance. Professional trainers have had long standing experience in avoiding the pitfalls of obedience training and can help you to avoid these mistakes as well. Doberman owners who have never trained a dog before have found, with professional assistance, their dog has become a super-star in obedience circles.

This training assistance can be obtained in many ways. Classes are particularly good for your Dobe's socialization. The dog will learn that he must obey even when there are other dogs and people around. These classes also keep the Doberman ever mindful of the fact that he must get along with other people and other dogs. There are free-of-charge classes at many parks and recreation facilities, as well as

Ch. Chalmar's The Big Red One, owned by Arnold Jacobson, holds bench, obedience and Schutzhund titles.

very formal and sometimes very expensive individual lessons with private trainers.

There are also some obedience schools that will take your Dobe and train him for you. A Doberman can and will learn with any good professional. However, unless your schedule provides no time at all to train your own dog, having someone else train the dog for you would be last on our list of recommendations. The rapport that develops between the owner who has trained his or her Dobe to be a pleasant companion and good canine citizen is very special—well worth the time and patience it requires to achieve.

VERSATILITY

The possibilities of sharing enjoyable experiences with your Doberman are endless. Dobermans seem to excel in just about anything a dog is capable of doing. The breed is probably one of the most versatile breeds of dog known to man.

Although not commonly known, Dobermans have proven to be outstanding hunters and herders. Their scenting and tracking abilities make them highly successful in both locating missing people and ferreting out narcotics.

Many Dobermans are used as therapy dogs for the aged or infirmed. It is amazing how gentle even the most robust young male can be with fragile people.

The breed has been of major assistance in both the World Wars as messenger and patrol dog. Dobermans are ideal performance and obedience dogs.

Protection

The Doberman Pinscher has a legendary reputation as a fearless natural protector. The Doberman owner's obligation is to build confidence in his or her dog. A confident companion dog will not bite indiscriminately. In order to enhance the protective capabilities of their Dobe, a responsible owner should undertake at least sixteen weeks of obedience training beginning when the puppy is six months old.

Additional training might include working toward Obedience titles such as Companion Dog Excellent, Utility Dog and Tracking Dog. Further, if the owner wishes to make the commitment, he or she can proceed on to Schutzhund training, which is the epitome of protection training. It must be understood, however, that Schutzhund training is very intensive and must only be done under the supervision of a trained professional.

Fun and Games

There are many opportunities for you to spend quality time with your Doberman that will provide exercise for both of you and valuable training for your dog. The AKC and UKC offer conformation and obedience classes, agility events and tracking tests. There is scent discrimination, hurdle racing, flyball, frisbee, weight pulling, and an endless array of hiking and backpacking activities.

Owning a Doberman is like having a best friend. This friend, however, loves doing anything and everything you enjoy, when and where you want to do it. Can you ask for more?

Slam dunk! The Doberman world's answer to Michael Jordan, HoMike Air Dragon, with basketball, jumps a five-foot fence with ease.

SPORT of Purebred Dogs

BY JUDY IBY

Welcome to the exciting and sometimes frustrating sport of dogs. No doubt you are trying to learn more about dogs or you wouldn't be deep into this book. This section covers the basics that may entice you, further your knowledge and help you to understand the dog world.

Dog showing has been a very popular sport for a long time and has been taken quite seriously by some. Others only enjoy it as a hobby.

The Kennel Club in England was formed in 1859, the American Kennel Club was established in 1884 and the Canadian Kennel Club was formed in 1888. The purpose of these clubs was to register purebred dogs and maintain their Stud Books. In the beginning, the concept of registering dogs was not readily accepted. More than 36 million dogs have been enrolled in the AKC Stud Book since its inception in 1888. Presently the kennel clubs not only register dogs but adopt and enforce rules and regulations governing dog shows, obedience trials and field trials. Over the years they have fostered and encouraged interest in the health and welfare of the purebred dog. They routinely donate funds to veterinary research for study on genetic disorders.

Below are the addresses of the kennel clubs in the United States, Great Britain and Canada.

Author Faye Strauss with Ch. Sherluck's Casalacia winning Best in Show at the Seattle Kennel Club.

The American Kennel Club
260 Madison Avenue
New York, NY 10016
(Their registry is located at: 5580 Centerview Drive, STE 200, Raleigh, NC 27606-3390)

SEATTLE KENNEL CLUB

BEST IN SHOW

The Kennel Club
1 Clarges Street
Piccadilly, London, W1Y 8AB, England

The Canadian Kennel Club
89 Skyway Avenue
Etobicoke, Ontario M9W 6R4
Canada

Today there are numerous activities that are enjoyable for both the dog and the handler. Some of the activities include conformation showing, obedience competition, tracking, agility, the Canine Good Citizen Certificate, and a wide range of instinct tests that vary from breed to breed. Where you start depends upon your goals which early on may not be readily apparent.

Every puppy can benefit from puppy kindergarten. It not only helps to produce a well-mannered companion, it is an excellent place to socialize your Doberman.

PUPPY KINDERGARTEN

Every puppy will benefit from this class. PKT is the foundation for all future dog activities from conformation to "couch potatoes." Pet owners should make an effort to attend even if they never expect to show their dog. The class is designed for puppies about three months of age with graduation at approximately five months of age. All the puppies will be in the same age group and, even though some may be a little unruly, there should not be any real problem. This class will teach the puppy some beginning obedience. As in all obedience classes the owner learns how to train his own dog. The PKT class gives the puppy the opportunity to interact

If you are a patient and flexible teacher, your Doberman is smart enough to learn even the most difficult of tricks.

with other puppies in the same age group and exposes him to strangers, which is very important. Some dogs grow up with behavior problems, one of them being fear of strangers. As you can see, there can be much to gain from this class.

There are some basic obedience exercises that every dog should learn. Some of these can be started with puppy kindergarten.

CONFORMATION

Conformation showing is our oldest dog show sport. This type of showing is based on the dog's appearance—that is his structure, movement and attitude. When considering this type of showing, you need to be aware of your breed's standard and be able to evaluate your dog compared to that standard. The breeder of your puppy or other experienced breeders would be good sources for such an evaluation. Puppies can go through lots of changes over a period of time. Many puppies start out as promising hopefuls and then after maturing may be disappointing as show candidates. Even so this should not deter them from being excellent pets.

Usually conformation training classes are offered by the local kennel or obedience clubs. These are excellent places for training puppies. The puppy should be able to walk on a lead before entering such a class. Proper ring procedure and technique for posing (stacking) the dog will be demonstrated as well as gaiting the dog. Usually certain patterns are used in the ring such as the triangle or the "L." Conformation class, like the PKT class, will give your youngster the opportunity to socialize with different breeds of dogs and humans too.

It takes some time to learn the routine of conformation showing. Usually one starts at the puppy matches that may be AKC Sanctioned or Fun Matches. These matches are generally for puppies from two or three months to a year old, and there may be classes for the adult over the age of 12 months. Similar to point shows, the classes are divided by sex and after completion of the classes in that breed or variety, the class winners compete for Best of Breed or Variety. The winner goes on to compete in the Group and the Group winners compete for Best in Match. No championship points are awarded for match wins.

A few matches can be great training for puppies even though there is no intention to go on showing. Matches enable the puppy to meet new people and be handled by a stranger—the judge. It is also a change of environment, which broadens the horizon for both dog and handler. Matches and other dog activities boost the confidence of the handler and especially the younger handlers.

Earning an AKC championship is built on a point system, which is different from Great Britain. To become an AKC Champion of Record the dog must earn 15 points. The number of points earned each time depends upon the number of dogs in competition. The number of points available at each show depends upon the breed, its sex and the location of the show. The United States is divided into ten AKC zones. Each zone has its own set of points. The purpose of the zones is to try to equalize the points available from breed to breed and area to area.The AKC adjusts the point scale annually.

The number of points that can be won at a show are between one and five. Three-, four- and five-point wins are considered majors. Not only does the dog need 15 points won under three different judges, but those points must include two majors under two different judges. Canada also works on a point system but majors are not required.

Dogs always show before bitches. The classes available to those seeking points are: Puppy (which may be divided into 6 to 9 months and 9 to 12 months); 12 to 18 months; Novice; Bred-by-Exhibitor; American-bred; and Open. The class winners of the same sex of each breed or variety compete against each other for Winners Dog and Winners Bitch. A Reserve Winners Dog and Reserve Winners Bitch are also awarded but do not carry any points unless the Winners win is disallowed by AKC. The Winners Dog and Bitch compete with the specials (those dogs that have attained championship) for Best of Breed or Variety, Best of Winners and Best of Opposite Sex. It is possible to pick up an extra point or even a major if the points are higher for the defeated winner than those of Best of Winners. The latter would get the higher total from the defeated winner.

Your Doberman Pinscher must be groomed perfectly if he is to participate in conformation.

At an all-breed show, each Best of Breed or Variety winner will go on to his respective Group and then the Group winners will compete against each other for Best in Show. There are seven Groups: Sporting, Hounds, Working, Terriers, Toys, Non-Sporting and Herding. Obviously there are no Groups at speciality shows (those shows that have only one breed or a show such as the American Spaniel Club's Flushing Spaniel Show, which is for all flushing spaniel breeds).

Earning a championship in England is somewhat different since they do not have a point system. Challenge Certificates are awarded if the judge feels the dog is deserving regardless of the number of dogs in competition. A dog must earn three Challenge Certificates under three different judges, with at least one of these Certificates being won after the age of 12 months. Competition is very strong and entries may be higher than they are in the U.S. The Kennel Club's Challenge Certificates are only available at Championship Shows.

In England, The Kennel Club regulations require that certain dogs, Border Collies and Gundog breeds, qualify in a working capacity (i.e., obedience or field trials) before becoming a full Champion. If they do not qualify in the working aspect, then they are designated a Show Champion, which is equivalent to the AKC's Champion of Record. A Gundog may be granted the title of Field Trial Champion (FT Ch.) if it passes all the tests in the field but would also have to qualify in conformation before becoming a full Champion. A Border Collie that earns the title of Obedience Champion (Ob Ch.) must also qualify in the conformation ring before becoming a Champion.

The U.S. doesn't have a designation full Champion but does award for Dual and Triple Champions. The Dual Champion must be a Champion of Record, and either Champion Tracker, Herding Champion, Obedience Trial Champion or Field Champion. Any dog that has been awarded the titles of Champion of Record, and any two of the following: Champion Tracker, Herding Champion, Obedience Trial Champion or Field Champion, may be designated as a Triple Champion.

The shows in England seem to put more emphasis on breeder judges than those in the U.S. There is much competition within the breeds. Therefore the quality of the individual breeds should be very good. In the United States we tend to have more "all around judges" (those that judge multiple breeds) and use the breeder judges at the specialty shows. Breeder judges are more familiar with their own breed since they are actively breeding that breed or did so at one time. Americans emphasize Group and Best in Show wins and promote them accordingly.

The shows in England can be very large and extend over several days, with the Groups being scheduled on different days. Though multi-day shows are not common in the U.S., there are cluster shows, where several different clubs will use the same show site over consecutive days.

Westminster Kennel Club is our most prestigious show although the entry is limited to 2500. In recent years, entry has been limited to Champions. This show is more formal than the majority of the shows with the judges wearing formal attire and the handlers fashionably dressed. In most instances the quality of the dogs is superb. After all, it is a show of Champions. It is a good show to study the AKC registered breeds and is by far the most exciting—especially since it is televised! WKC is one of the few shows in this country that is still benched. This means the dog must be in his benched area during the show hours except when he is being groomed, in the ring, or being exercised.

The versatile Doberman can participate in many different activities. This Dobe easily flies over the bar jump.

Typically, the handlers are very particular about their appearances. They are careful not to wear

something that will detract from their dog but will perhaps enhance it. American ring procedure is quite formal compared to that of other countries. There is a certain etiquette expected between the judge and exhibitor and among the other exhibitors. Of course it is not always the case but the judge is supposed to be polite, not engaging in small talk or acknowledging how well he knows the handler. There is a more informal and relaxed atmosphere at the shows in other countries. For instance, the dress code is more casual. I can see where this might be more fun for the exhibitor and especially for the novice. The U.S. is very handler-oriented in many of the breeds. It is true, in most instances, that the experienced professional handler can present the dog better and will have a feel for what a judge likes.

In England, Crufts is The Kennel Club's own show and is most assuredly the largest dog show in the world. They've been known to have an entry of nearly 20,000, and the show lasts four days. Entry is only gained by qualifying through winning in specified classes at another Championship Show. Westminster is strictly conformation, but Crufts exhibitors and spectators enjoy not only conformation but obedience, agility and a multitude of exhibitions as well. Obedience was admitted in 1957 and agility in 1983.

If you are handling your own dog, please give some consideration to your apparel. For sure the dress code at matches is more informal than the point shows. However, you

The time you spend with your Doberman on training exercises will create a close bond between dog and owner.

should wear something a little more appropriate than beach attire or ragged jeans and bare feet. If you check out the handlers and see what is presently fashionable, you'll catch on. Men usually dress with a shirt and tie and a

The Westminster Kennel Club Dog Show is the most prestigious in the United States. It is held in New York City annually.

nice sports coat. Whether you are male or female, you will want to wear comfortable clothes and shoes. You need to be able to run with your dog and you certainly don't want to take a chance of falling and hurting yourself. Heaven forbid, if nothing else, you'll upset your dog. Women usually wear a dress or two-piece outfit, preferably with pockets to carry bait, comb, brush, etc. In this case men are the lucky ones with all their pockets. Ladies, think about where your dress will be if you need to kneel on the floor and also think about running. Does it allow freedom to do so?

You need to take along dog; crate; ex pen (if you use one); extra newspaper; water pail and water; all required grooming equipment, including hair dryer and extension cord; table; chair for you; bait for dog and lunch for you and friends; and, last but not least, clean up materials, such as plastic bags, paper towels, and perhaps a bath towel and some shampoo— just in case. Don't forget your entry confirmation and directions to the show.

If you are showing in obedience, then you will want to wear pants. Many of our top obedience handlers wear pants that are color-coordinated with their dogs. The philosophy is that imperfections in the black dog will be less obvious next to your black pants.

Whether you are showing in conformation, Junior Showmanship or obedience, you need to watch the clock and be sure you are not late. It is customary to pick up your conformation armband a few minutes before the start of the class. They will not wait for you and if you are on the show grounds and not in the ring, you will upset everyone. It's a little more complicated picking up your obedience armband if you show later in the class. If you have not picked up your armband and they get to your number, you may not be allowed to show. It's best to pick up your armband early, but then you may show earlier than expected if other handlers don't pick up. Customarily all conflicts should be discussed with the judge prior to the start of the class.

Junior Showmanship

The Junior Showmanship Class is a wonderful way to build self confidence even if there are no aspirations of staying with the dog-show game later in life. Frequently, Junior Showmanship becomes the background of those who become successful exhibitors/handlers in the future. In some instances it is taken very seriously, and success is measured in terms of wins. The Junior Handler is judged solely on his ability and skill in presenting his dog. The dog's conformation is not to be considered by the judge. Even so the condition and grooming of the dog may be a reflection upon the handler.

Usually the matches and point shows include different classes. The Junior Handler's dog may be entered in a breed or obedience class and even shown by another person in that class. Junior Showmanship classes are usually divided by age and perhaps sex. The age is determined by the handler's age on the day of the show. The classes are:

In order for your dog to pass the Canine Good Citizen Test, he must get along with people of all ages. These Dobe pups are on their way to good citizenship!

96

To the victor goes the spoils! This beautiful Doberman takes Best in Show.

CANINE GOOD CITIZEN

The AKC sponsors a program to encourage dog owners to train their dogs. Local clubs perform the pass/fail tests, and dogs who pass are awarded a Canine Good Citizen Certificate. Proof of vaccination is required at the time of participation. The test includes:

1. Accepting a friendly stranger.
2. Sitting politely for petting.
3. Appearance and grooming.
4. Walking on a loose leash.
5. Walking through a crowd.
6. Sit and down on command/staying in place.
7. Come when called.
8. Reaction to another dog.
9. Reactions to distractions.
10. Supervised separation.

If more effort was made by pet owners to accomplish these exercises, fewer dogs would be cast off to the humane shelter.

OBEDIENCE

Obedience is necessary, without a doubt, but it can also become a wonderful hobby or even an obsession. Obedience classes and competition can provide wonderful companionship, not only with your dog but with your classmates or fellow competitors. It is always gratifying to discuss your dog's problems with others who have had similar experiences. The AKC acknowledged Obedience around 1936, and it has changed tremendously even though many of the exercises are basically the same. Today, obedience competition is just that—very competitive. Even so, it is possible for every obedience exhibitor to come home a winner (by earning qualifying scores) even though he/she may not earn a placement in the class.

Most of the obedience titles are awarded after earning three qualifying scores (legs) in the appropriate class under three different judges. These classes offer a perfect score of 200, which is extremely rare. Each of the class exercises has its own point value. A leg is earned after receiving a score of at least 170 and at least 50 percent of the points available in each exercise. The titles are:

Companion Dog—CD

Companion Dog Excellent—CDX

Utility Dog—UD

After achieving the UD title, you may feel inclined to go after the UDX and/or OTCh. The UDX (Utility Dog Excellent) title went into effect in January 1994. It is not easily attained. The title requires qualifying simultaneously ten times in Open B and Utility B but not necessarily at consecutive shows.

The OTCh (Obedience Trial Champion) is awarded after the dog has earned his UD and then goes on to earn 100 championship points, a first place in Utility, a first place in Open and another first place in either class. The placements must be won under three different judges at all-breed obedience trials. The points are determined by the number of dogs competing in the Open B and Utility B classes. The OTCh title precedes the dog's name.

Obedience matches (AKC Sanctioned, Fun, and Show and Go) are usually available. Usually they are sponsored by the local obedience clubs. When preparing an obedience dog for a title, you will find matches very helpful. Fun Matches and Show and Go Matches are more lenient in allowing you to make corrections in the ring. This type of training is usually very necessary for the Open and Utility Classes. AKC Sanctioned Obedience Matches do not allow corrections in the ring since they must abide by the AKC Obedience Regulations. If you are interested in showing in obedience, then you should contact the AKC for a copy of the Obedience Regulations.

TRACKING

Tracking is officially classified obedience. There are three tracking titles available: Tracking Dog (TD), Tracking Dog Excellent (TDX), Variable Surface Tracking (VST). If all three tracking titles are obtained, then the dog officially becomes a CT (Champion Tracker). The CT will go in front of the dog's name.

There are few obstacles a well-trained Doberman, such as Udo's Jazz v. Ryansluxus, is unable to surmount.

A TD may be earned anytime and does not have to follow the other obedience titles. There are many exhibitors that prefer tracking to obedience, and there are others who do both. In my experience with small dogs, I prefer to earn the CD and CDX before attempting tracking. My reasoning is that small dogs are closer to the mat in the obedience rings and therefore it's too easy to put the nose down and sniff. Tracking encourages sniffing. Of course this depends on the dog. I've had some dogs that tracked around the ring and others (TDXs) who wouldn't think of sniffing in the ring.

AGILITY

Agility was first introduced by John Varley in England at the Crufts Dog Show, February 1978, but Peter Meanwell, competitor and judge, actually developed the idea. It was officially recognized in the early '80s. Agility is extremely popular in England and Canada and growing in popularity in the

U.S. The AKC acknowledged agility in August 1994. Dogs must be at least 12 months of age to be entered. It is a fascinating sport that the dog, handler and spectators enjoy to the utmost. Agility is a spectator sport! The dog performs off lead. The handler either runs with his dog or positions himself on the course and directs his dog with verbal and hand signals over a timed course over or through a variety of obstacles including a time out or pause. One of the main drawbacks to

Kathy and Mike Horniman's U-Ach., Ch. BJF Much Ado About Nothing, CDX, ROM, TDI, NA, VCX, otherwise known as Betty, is an extremely accomplished Doberman.

agility is finding a place to train. The obstacles take up a lot of space and it is very time consuming to put up and take down courses.

The titles earned at AKC agility trials are Novice Agility Dog (NAD), Open Agility Dog (OAD), Agility Dog Excellent (ADX), and Master Agility Excellent (MAX). In order to acquire an agility title, a dog must earn a qualifying score in its respective class on three separate occasions under two different judges. The MAX will be awarded after earning ten qualifying scores in the Agility Excellent Class.

PERFORMANCE TESTS

During the last decade the American Kennel Club has promoted performance tests—those events that test the different breeds' natural abilities. This type of event encourages a handler to devote even more time to his dog and retain the natural instincts of his breed heritage. It is an important part of the wonderful world of dogs.

SCHUTZHUND

The German word "Schutzhund" translated to English means "Protection Dog." It is a fast growing competitive sport in

HoMike's Erick Main pulls a cart in the annual town parade. He is an outstanding agility dog and a certified therapy dog.

Agility is an exciting sport, not only for the dogs, but for the spectators as well. Five-year-old Betty clears the window jump.

the United States and has been popular in England since the early 1900s. Schutzhund was originally a test to determine which German Shepherds were quality dogs for breeding in Germany. It gives us the ability to test our dogs for correct temperament and working ability. Like every other dog sport, it requires teamwork between the handler and the dog.

Schutzhund training and showing involves three phases: Tracking, Obedience and Protection. There are three SchH levels: SchH I (novice), SchH II (intermediate), and SchH III (advanced). Each title becomes progressively more difficult. The handler and dog start out in each phase with 100 points. Points are deducted as errors are incurred. A total perfect score is 300, and for a dog and handler to earn a title he must earn at least 70 points in tracking and obedience and at least 80 points in protection. Today many different breeds participate successfully in Schutzhund.

GENERAL INFORMATION

Obedience, tracking and agility allow the purebred dog with an Indefinite Listing Privilege (ILP) number or a limited registration to be exhibited and earn titles. Application must be made to the AKC for an ILP number.

The American Kennel Club publishes a monthly *Events* magazine that is part of the *Gazette*, their official journal for the sport of purebred dogs. The *Events* section lists upcoming shows and the secretary or superintendent for them. The majority of the conformation shows in the U.S. are overseen by licensed superintendents. Generally the entry closing date is approximately two-and-a-half weeks before the actual show. Point shows are fairly expensive, while the match

Craig Lanham, a certified trainer at the Lower Richland Schutzhund Club in Canada, puts a well-trained Doberman through his paces.

shows cost about one third of the point show entry fee. Match shows usually take entries the day of the show but some are pre-entry. The best way to find match show information is through your local kennel club. Upon asking, the AKC can provide you with a list of superintendents, and you can write and ask to be put on their mailing lists.

Obedience trial and tracking test information is available through the AKC. Frequently these events are not superintended, but put on by the host club. Therefore you would make the entry with the event's secretary.

As you have read, there are numerous activities you can share with your dog. Regardless what you do, it does take teamwork. Your dog can only benefit from your attention and training. We hope this chapter has enlightened you and hope, if nothing else, you will attend a show here and there. Perhaps you will start with a puppy kindergarten class, and who knows where it may lead!

HEALTH CARE

Veterinary medicine has become far more sophisticated than what was available to our ancestors. This can be attributed to the increase in household pets and consequently the demand for better care for them. Also human medicine has become far more complex. Today diagnostic testing in veterinary medicine parallels human diagnostics. Because of better technology we can expect our pets to live healthier lives thereby increasing their life spans.

The health of your Doberman Pinscher depends on your consistent care and the regular care of a veterinarian.

THE FIRST CHECK UP

You will want to take your new puppy/dog in for its first check up within 48 to 72 hours after acquiring it. Many breeders strongly recommend this check up and so do the humane shelters. A puppy/dog can appear healthy but it may have a serious problem that is not apparent to the layman. Most pets have some type of a minor flaw that may never cause a real problem.

Unfortunately if he/she should have a serious problem, you will want to consider the consequences of keeping the pet and the attachments that will be formed, which may be broken prematurely. Keep in mind there are many healthy dogs looking for good homes.

Proper health care from the start will ensure that this young puppy will live a long and active life.

104

This first check up is a good time to establish yourself with the veterinarian and learn the office policy regarding their hours and how they handle emergencies. Usually the breeder or another conscientious pet owner is a good reference for locating a capable veterinarian. You should be aware that not all veterinarians give the same quality of service. Please do not make your selection on the least expensive clinic, as they may be short changing your pet. There is the possibility that eventually it will cost you more due to improper diagnosis, treatment, etc. If you are selecting a new veterinarian, feel free to ask for a tour of the clinic. You should inquire about making an appointment for a tour since all clinics are working clinics, and therefore may not be available all day for sightseers. You may worry less if you see where your pet will be spending the day if he ever needs to be hospitalized.

Vaccinations are necessary to protect your pup from life-threatening diseases. Your veterinarian will put your Doberman on an immunization schedule.

THE PHYSICAL EXAM

Your veterinarian will check your pet's overall condition, which includes listening to the heart; checking the respiration; feeling the abdomen, muscles and joints; checking the mouth, which includes the gum color and signs of gum disease along with plaque buildup; checking the ears for signs of an infection or ear mites; examining the eyes; and, last but not least, checking the condition of the skin and coat.

He should ask you questions regarding your pet's eating and elimination habits and invite you to relay your questions. It is a good idea to prepare a list so as not to forget anything. He should discuss the proper diet and the quantity to be fed. If this should differ from your breeder's recommendation, then you should convey to him the breeder's choice and see if he approves. If he recommends changing the diet, then this should be done over a few days so as not to cause a gastrointestinal upset. It is customary to take in a fresh stool

A thorough oral exam should be part of your Doberman Pinscher's regular check-up.

sample (just a small amount) for a test for intestinal parasites. It must be fresh, preferably within 12 hours, since the eggs hatch quickly and after hatching will not be observed under the microscope. If your pet isn't obliging then, usually the technician can take one in the clinic.

IMMUNIZATIONS

It is important that you take your puppy/dog's vaccination record with you on your first visit. In case of a puppy, presumably the breeder has seen to the vaccinations up to the time you acquired custody. Veterinarians differ in their vaccination protocol. It is not unusual for your puppy to have received vaccinations for distemper, hepatitis, leptospirosis, parvovirus and parainfluenza every two to three weeks from the age of five or six weeks. Usually this is a combined injection and is typically called the DHLPP. The DHLPP is given through at least 12 to 14 weeks of age, and it is customary to continue with another parvovirus vaccine at 16 to 18 weeks. You may wonder why so many immunizations are necessary. No one knows for sure when the puppy's maternal antibodies are gone, although it is customarily accepted that distemper antibodies are gone by 12 weeks. Usually parvovirus antibodies are gone by 16 to 18 weeks of age. However, it is possible for the maternal antibodies to be gone at a much earlier age or even a later age. Therefore immunizations are started at an early age. The vaccine will not give immunity as long as there are maternal antibodies.

The rabies vaccination is given at three or six months of age depending on your local laws. A vaccine for bordetella (kennel cough) is advisable and can be given anytime from the age of five weeks. The coronavirus is not commonly given unless there is a problem locally. The Lyme vaccine is necessary in endemic areas. Lyme disease has been reported in 47 states.

Distemper

This is virtually an incurable disease. If the dog recovers, he is subject to severe nervous disorders. The virus attacks every tissue in the body and resembles a bad cold with a fever. It can cause a runny nose and eyes and cause gastrointestinal disorders, including a poor appetite, vomiting and diarrhea. The virus is carried by raccoons, foxes, wolves, mink and other dogs. Unvaccinated youngsters and senior citizens are very susceptible. This is still a common disease.

Hepatitis

This is a virus that is most serious in very young dogs. It is spread by contact with an infected animal or its stool or urine. The virus affects the liver and kidneys and is characterized by high fever, depression and lack of appetite. Recovered animals may be afflicted with chronic illnesses.

Leptospirosis

This is a bacterial disease transmitted by contact with the urine of an infected dog, rat or other wildlife. It produces severe symptoms of fever, depression, jaundice and internal bleeding and was fatal before the vaccine was developed. Recovered dogs can be carriers, and the disease can be transmitted from dogs to humans.

Parvovirus

This was first noted in the late 1970s and is still a fatal disease. However, with proper vaccinations, early diagnosis and prompt treatment, it is a manageable disease. It attacks the bone marrow and intestinal tract. The symptoms include depression, loss of appetite, vomiting, diarrhea and collapse. Immediate medical attention is of the essence.

Rabies

This is shed in the saliva and is carried by raccoons, skunks, foxes, other dogs and cats. It attacks nerve tissue, resulting in paralysis and death. Rabies can be transmitted to people and is virtually always fatal. This disease is reappearing in the suburbs.

Annual booster shots will be necessary throughout the life of your dog.

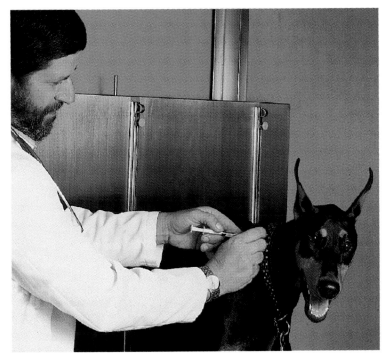

Bordetella (Kennel Cough)

The symptoms are coughing, sneezing, hacking and retching accompanied by nasal discharge usually lasting from a few days to several weeks. There are several disease-producing organisms responsible for this disease. The present vaccines are helpful but do not protect for all the strains. It usually is not life threatening but in some instances it can progress to a serious bronchopneumonia. The disease is highly contagious. The vaccination should be given routinely for dogs that come in contact with other dogs, such as through boarding, training class or visits to the groomer.

Coronavirus

This is usually self limiting and not life threatening. It was first noted in the late '70s about a year before parvovirus. The virus produces a yellow/brown stool and there may be depression, vomiting and diarrhea.

Lyme Disease

This was first diagnosed in the United States in 1976 in Lyme, CT in people who lived in close proximity to the deer tick. Symptoms may include acute lameness, fever, swelling of joints and loss of appetite. Your veterinarian can advise you if you live in an endemic area.

After your puppy has completed his puppy vaccinations, you will continue to booster the DHLPP once a year. It is

Bordetella attached to canine cilia. Otherwise known as kennel cough, this disease is highly contagious and should be vaccinated against routinely.

customary to booster the rabies one year after the first vaccine and then, depending on where you live, it should be boostered every year or every three years. This depends on your local laws. The Lyme and corona vaccines are boostered annually and it is recommended that the bordetella be boostered every six to eight months.

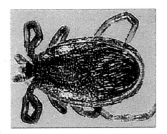

The deer tick is the most common carrier of Lyme disease. Photo courtesy of Virbac Laboratories, Inc., Fort Worth, Texas.

ANNUAL VISIT

I would like to impress the importance of the annual check up, which would include the booster vaccinations, check for intestinal parasites and test for heartworm. Today in our very busy world it is rush, rush and see "how much you can get for how little." Unbelievably, some non-veterinary businesses have entered into the vaccination business. More harm than good can come to your dog through improper vaccinations, possibly from inferior vaccines and/or the wrong schedule. More than likely you truly care about your companion dog and over the years you have devoted much time and expense to his well being. Perhaps you are unaware that a vaccination is not just a vaccination. There is more involved. Please, please follow through with regular physical examinations. It is so important for your veterinarian to know your dog and this is especially true during middle age through the geriatric years. More than likely your older dog will require more than one physical a year. The annual physical is good preventive medicine. Through early diagnosis and subsequent treatment your dog can maintain a longer and better quality of life.

INTESTINAL PARASITES

Hookworms

These are almost microscopic intestinal worms that can cause anemia and therefore serious problems, including death, in young puppies. Hookworms can be transmitted to humans through penetration of the skin. Puppies may be born with them.

Roundworms

These are spaghetti-like worms that can cause a potbellied appearance and dull coat along with more severe symptoms, such as vomiting, diarrhea and coughing. Puppies acquire these while in the mother's uterus and through lactation. Both hookworms and roundworms may be acquired through ingestion.

Whipworms

These have a three-month life cycle and are not acquired through the dam. They cause intermittent diarrhea usually with mucus. Whipworms are possibly the most difficult worm to eradicate. Their eggs are very resistant to most environmental factors and can last for years until the proper conditions enable them to mature. Whipworms are seldom seen in the stool.

Intestinal parasites are more prevalent in some areas than others. Climate, soil and contamination are big factors contributing to the incidence of intestinal parasites. Eggs are passed in the stool, lay on the ground and then become infective in a certain number of days. Each of the above worms has a different life cycle. Your best chance of becoming and remaining worm-free is to always pooper-scoop your yard. A fenced-in yard keeps stray dogs out, which is certainly helpful.

I would recommend having a fecal examination on your dog twice a year or more often if there is a problem. If your dog has a positive fecal sample, then he will be given the appropriate medication and you will be asked to bring back another stool sample in a certain period of time (depending on the type of worm) and then be rewormed. This process goes on until he

Whipworms can be very hard to find— a task best left to a veterinarian. Pictured here are adult whipworms.

has at least two negative samples. The different types of worms require different medications. You will be wasting your money and doing your dog an injustice by buying over-the-counter medication without first consulting your veterinarian.

OTHER INTERNAL PARASITES

Coccidiosis and Giardiasis
These protozoal infections

There are many parasites lurking about that your Doberman Pinscher may pick up when outdoors. Be sure to check his coat thoroughly after playing outside.

Roundworm eggs, as would be seen on a fecal evaluation. The eggs must develop for at least 12 days before they are infective.

usually affect puppies, especially in places where large numbers of

puppies are brought together. Older dogs may harbor these infections but do not show signs unless they are stressed. Symptoms include diarrhea, weight loss and lack of appetite. These infections are not always apparent in the fecal examination.

Tapeworms

Seldom apparent on fecal floatation, they are diagnosed frequently as rice-like segments around the dog's anus and the base of the tail. Tapeworms are long, flat and ribbon like, sometimes several feet in length, and made up of many segments about five-eighths of an inch long. The two most common types of tapeworms found in the dog are:

(1) First the larval form of the flea tapeworm parasite must mature in an intermediate host, the flea, before it can become infective. Your dog acquires this by ingesting the flea through licking and chewing.

Worms can be passed from dam to puppy. Usually it is best to assume that all puppies have worms and treat them.

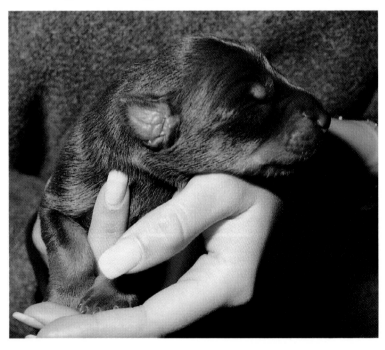

(2) Rabbits, rodents and certain large game animals serve as intermediate hosts for other species of tapeworms. If your dog should eat one of these infected hosts, then he can acquire tapeworms.

HEARTWORM DISEASE

This is a worm that resides in the heart and adjacent blood vessels of the lung that produces microfilaria, which circulate in the bloodstream. It is possible for a dog to be infected with any number of worms from one to a hundred that can be 6 to 14 inches long. It is a life-threatening disease, expensive to treat and easily prevented. Depending on where you live, your veterinarian may recommend a preventive year-round and either an annual or semiannual blood test. The most common preventive is given once a month.

The cat flea is the most common flea of both cats and dogs. Courtesy of Fleabusters, Rx for Fleas, Inc., Fort Lauderdale, Florida.

EXTERNAL PARASITES

Fleas

These pests are not only the dog's worst enemy but also enemy to the owner's pocketbook. Preventing is less expensive than treating, but regardless we'd prefer to spend our money elsewhere. Likely, the majority of our dogs are allergic to the bite of a flea, and in many cases it only takes one flea bite. The protein in the flea's saliva is the culprit. Allergic dogs have a reaction, which usually results in a "hot spot." More than likely such a reaction will involve a trip to the veterinarian for treatment. Yes, prevention is less expensive. Fortunately today there are several good products available.

If there is a flea infestation, no one product is going to correct the problem. Not only will the dog require treatment so will the environment. In general flea collars are not very effective although there is now available an "egg" collar that will kill the eggs on the dog. Dips are the most economical but

they are messy. There are some effective shampoos and treatments available through pet shops and veterinarians. An oral tablet arrived on the American market in 1995 and was popular in Europe the previous year. It sterilizes the female flea but will not kill adult fleas. Therefore the tablet, which is given monthly, will decrease the flea population but is not a "cure-all." Those dogs that suffer from flea-bite allergy will still be subjected to the bite of the flea. Another popular parasiticide is permethrin, which is applied to the back of the dog in one or two places depending on the dog's weight. This product works as a repellent causing the flea to get "hot feet" and jump off. Do not confuse this product with some of the organophosphates that are also applied to the dog's back.

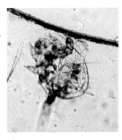

Sarcoptes are highly contagious to other dogs and to humans, although they do not live long on humans. They cause intense itching.

Some products are not usable on young puppies. Treating fleas should be done under your veterinarian's guidance. Frequently it is necessary to combine products and the layman does not have the knowledge regarding possible toxicities. It is hard to believe but there are a few dogs that do have a natural resistance to fleas. Nevertheless it would be wise to treat all pets at the same time. Don't forget your cats. Cats just love to prowl the neighborhood and consequently return with unwanted guests.

Adult fleas live on the dog but their eggs drop off the dog into the environment. There they go through four larval stages before reaching adulthood, and thereby are able to jump back on the poor unsuspecting dog. The cycle resumes and takes between 21 to 28 days under ideal conditions. There are environmental products available that will kill both the adult fleas and the larvae.

Doberman pups are vulnerable when outside to fleas, ticks and other parasites. Check his coat carefully after playing outdoors.

Ticks

Ticks carry Rocky Mountain Spotted Fever, Lyme disease and can cause tick paralysis. They should be removed with tweezers, trying to pull out the head. The jaws carry disease. There is a tick preventive collar that does an excellent job. The ticks automatically back out on those dogs wearing collars.

Sarcoptic Mange

This is a mite that is difficult to find on skin scrapings. The pinnal reflex is a good indicator of this disease. Rub the ends of the pinna (ear) together and the dog will start scratching with his foot. Sarcoptes are highly contagious to other dogs and to humans although they do not live long on humans. They cause intense itching.

Demodectic Mange

This is a mite that is passed from the dam to her puppies. It affects youngsters age three to ten months. Diagnosis is confirmed by skin scraping. Small areas of alopecia around the eyes, lips and/or forelegs become visible. There is little itching unless there is a secondary bacterial infection. Some breeds are afflicted more than others.

Cheyletiella

This causes intense itching and is diagnosed by skin scraping. It lives in the outer layers of the skin of dogs, cats, rabbits and humans. Yellow-gray scales may be found on the back and the rump, top of the head and the nose.

To Breed or Not To Breed

More than likely your breeder has requested that you have your puppy neutered or spayed. Your breeder's request is based on what is healthiest for your dog and what is most beneficial for your breed. Experienced and conscientious breeders devote many years into developing a bloodline. In order to do this, he makes every effort to plan each breeding in regard to conformation, temperament and health. This type of breeder does his best to perform the necessary testing (i.e., OFA, CERF, testing for inherited blood disorders, thyroid, etc.). Testing is expensive and sometimes very disheartening when a favorite dog doesn't pass his health tests. The health history pertains not only to the breeding stock but to the immediate ancestors. Reputable breeders do not want their offspring to be bred indiscriminately. Therefore you may be asked to neuter or spay your puppy. Of course there is always the exception, and your breeder may agree to let you breed your dog under his direct supervision. This is an important concept. More and more effort is being made to breed healthier dogs.

Spay/Neuter

There are numerous benefits of performing this surgery at six months of age. Unspayed females are subject to mammary and ovarian cancer. In order to prevent mammary cancer she must be spayed prior to her first heat cycle. Later in life, an unspayed female may develop a pyometra (an infected uterus), which is definitely life threatening.

Spaying is performed under a general anesthetic and is easy on the young dog. As you might expect it is a little harder on the older dog, but that is no reason to deny her the surgery.

Breeding your dog is a huge responsibility and something that should not be entered into lightly. This Doberman mother divides her affection between her owner and her pups.

The surgery removes the ovaries and uterus. It is important to remove all the ovarian tissue. If some is left behind, she could remain attractive to males. In order to view the ovaries, a reasonably long incision is necessary. An ovariohysterectomy is considered major surgery.

Neutering the male at a young age will inhibit some characteristic male behavior that owners frown upon. Some boys will not hike their legs and mark territory if they are neutered at six months of age. Also neutering at a young age has hormonal benefits, lessening the chance of hormonal aggressiveness.

Your Doberman Pinscher will need annual check-ups to maintain his good health and minimize any future problems.

Surgery involves removing the testicles but leaving the scrotum. If there should be a retained testicle, then he definitely needs to be neutered before the age of two or three years. Retained testicles can develop into cancer. Unneutered males are at risk for testicular cancer, perineal fistulas, perianal tumors and fistulas and prostatic disease.

Intact males and females are prone to housebreaking accidents. Females urinate frequently before, during and after heat cycles, and males tend to mark territory if there is a female in heat. Males may show the same behavior if there is a visiting dog or guests.

Surgery involves a sterile operating procedure equivalent to human surgery. The incision site is shaved, surgically scrubbed and draped. The veterinarian wears a sterile surgical gown, cap, mask and gloves. Anesthesia should be monitored by a registered technician. It is customary for the veterinarian to recommend a pre-anesthetic blood screening, looking for metabolic problems and a ECG rhythm strip to check for normal heart function. Today anesthetics are equal to human anesthetics, which enables your dog to walk out of the clinic the same day as surgery.

Some folks worry about their dog gaining weight after being neutered or spayed. This is usually not the case. It is true that some dogs may be less active so they could develop a problem, but most dogs are just as active as they were before surgery. However, if your dog should begin to gain, then you need to decrease his food and see to it that he gets a little more exercise.

Most Dobermans have proven to be kind, loving and extremely tolerant mothers.

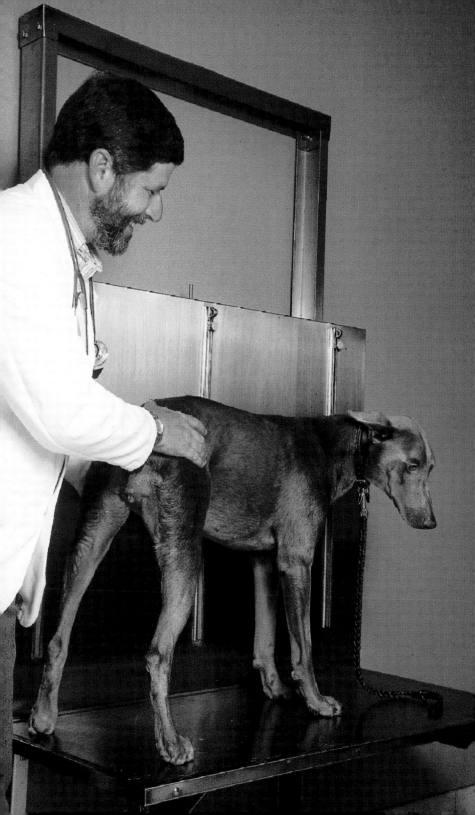

DENTAL CARE for Your Dog's Life

So you've got a new puppy! You also have a new set of puppy teeth in your household. Anyone who has ever raised a puppy is abundantly aware of these new teeth. Your puppy will chew anything it can reach, chase your shoelaces, and play "tear the rag" with any piece of clothing it can find. When puppies are newly born, they have no teeth. At about four weeks of age, puppies of most breeds begin to develop their deciduous or baby teeth. They begin eating semi-solid food, fighting and biting with their litter mates, and learning discipline from their mother. As their new teeth come in, they inflict more pain on their mother's breasts, so her feeding sessions become less frequent and shorter. By six or eight weeks, the mother will start growling to warn her pups when they are fighting too roughly or hurting her as they nurse too much with their new teeth.

All dogs need safe chew toys to keep their teeth and jaws occupied. Chewing removes plaque and tartar and helps keep your pup's mouth clean.

Puppies need to chew. It is a necessary part of their physical and mental development. They develop muscles and necessary life skills as they drag objects around, fight over possession, and vocalize alerts and warnings. Puppies chew on things to explore their world. They are using their sense of taste to determine what is food and what is not. How else can they tell an electrical cord from a lizard? At about four months of age, most puppies begin shedding their baby teeth. Often these teeth need some help

Make sure your Doberman puppies always have plenty of Nylabones® to choose from.

to come out and make way for the permanent teeth. The incisors (front teeth) will be replaced first. Then, the adult canine or fang teeth erupt. When the baby tooth is not shed before the permanent tooth comes in, veterinarians call it a retained deciduous tooth. This condition will often cause gum infections by trapping hair and debris between the permanent tooth and the retained baby tooth. Nylafloss® is an excellent device for puppies to use. They can toss it, drag it, and chew on the many surfaces it presents. The baby teeth can catch in the nylon material, aiding in their removal. Puppies that have adequate chew toys will have less destructive behavior, develop more physically, and have less chance of retained deciduous teeth.

During the first year, your dog should be seen by your veterinarian at regular intervals. Your veterinarian will let you know when to bring in your puppy for vaccinations and parasite examinations. At each visit, your

Provide your pups with plenty of safe chew toys or they might decide to use your sneaker instead!

Your Doberman will thrive with good health care, nutrition, and grooming, which includes safe treats and regular oral checkups.

veterinarian should inspect the lips, teeth, and mouth as part of a complete physical examination. You should take some part in the maintenance of your dog's oral health. You should examine your dog's mouth weekly throughout his first year to make sure there are no sores, foreign objects, tooth problems, etc. If your dog drools excessively, shakes its head, or has bad breath, consult your veterinarian. By the time your dog is six months old, the permanent teeth are all in and plaque can start to accumulate on the tooth surfaces. This is when your dog needs to develop good dental-care habits to prevent calculus build-up on its teeth. Brushing is best. That is a fact that cannot be denied. However, some dogs do not like their teeth brushed regularly, or you may not be able to accomplish the task. In that case, you should consider a product that will help prevent plaque and calculus build-up.

The Plaque Attackers® and Galileo Bone® are other excellent choices for the first three years of a dog's life. Their shapes make them interesting for the dog. As the dog chews on them, the solid polyurethane massages the gums which improves the blood circulation to the periodontal tissues. Projections on the chew devices increase the surface and are in contact with the tooth for more efficient cleaning. The unique shape and consistency prevent your dog from exerting excessive force on his own teeth or from breaking off pieces of the bone. If your dog is an aggressive chewer or weighs more than 55 pounds (25 kg), you should consider giving him a Nylabone®, the most durable chew product on the market.

The Gumabones ®, made by the Nylabone Company, is constructed of strong polyurethane, which is softer than nylon. Less powerful chewers prefer the Gumabones® to the Nylabones®. A super option for your dog is the Hercules Bone®, a uniquely shaped bone named after the great Olympian for its exception strength. Like all Nylabone products, they are specially scented to make them attractive to your dog. Ask your veterinarian about these bones and he will validate the good doctor's prescription: Nylabones® not only give your dog a good chewing workout but also help to save your dog's teeth (and even his life, as it protects him from possible fatal periodontal diseases).

By the time dogs are four years old, 75% of them have periodontal disease. It is the most common infection in dogs. Yearly examinations by your veterinarian are essential to maintaining your dog's good health. If your veterinarian detects periodontal disease, he or she may recommend a prophylactic cleaning. To do a thorough cleaning, it will be necessary to put your dog under anesthesia. With modern gas anesthetics and monitoring equipment, the procedure is pretty safe. Your veterinarian will scale the teeth with an ultrasound

Your Doberman will enjoy hours of fun with Nylafloss®, a great tug toy that will literally floss his teeth while he plays.

scaler or hand instrument. This removes the calculus from the teeth. If there are calculus deposits below the gum line, the veterinarian will plane the roots to make them smooth. After all of the calculus has been removed, the teeth are polished with pumice in a polishing cup. If any medical or surgical treatment is needed, it is done at this time.

Good oral care is important to your dog's health and well-being. If you start your puppy on the road to good health, his teeth will last a lifetime.

As aggressive chewers, it is important to provide your Doberman with toys he cannot easily shatter or swallow.

The final step would be fluoride treatment and your follow-up treatment at home. If the periodontal disease is

advanced, the veterinarian may prescribe a medicated mouth rinse or antibiotics for use at home. Make sure your dog has safe, clean and attractive chew toys and treats. Chooz® treats are another way of using a consumable treat to help keep your dog's teeth clean.

Rawhide is the most popular of all materials for a dog to chew. This has never been good news to dog owners, because rawhide is inherently very dangerous for dogs. Thousands of dogs have died from rawhide, having swallowed the hide after it has become soft and mushy, only to cause stomach and intestinal blockage. A new rawhide product on the market has finally solved the problem of rawhide: molded Roar-Hide® from Nylabone. These are composed of processed, cut up, and melted American rawhide injected into your dog's favorite shape: a dog bone. These dog-safe devices smell and taste like rawhide but don't break up. The ridges on the bones help to fight tartar build-up on the teeth and they last ten times longer than the usual rawhide chews.

Check your Doberman's teeth and mouth as part of his regular grooming routine.

Safe toys can help curb behavior problems such as chewing and barking.

As your dog ages, professional examination and cleaning should become more frequent. The mouth should be inspected at least once a year. Your veterinarian may recommend visits every six months. In the geriatric patient, organs such as the heart, liver, and kidneys do not function as well as when they were young. Your veterinarian will probably want to test these organs' functions prior to using general anesthesia for dental cleaning. If your dog is a good chewer and you work closely with your veterinarian, your dog can keep all of its teeth all of its life. However, as your dog ages, his sense of smell, sight, and taste will diminish. He may not have the desire to chase, trap or chew his toys. He will also not have the energy to chew for long periods, as arthritis and periodontal disease make chewing painful. This will leave you with more responsibility for keeping his teeth clean and healthy. The dog that would not let you brush his teeth at one year of age, may let you brush his teeth now that he is ten years old.

If you train your dog with good chewing habits as a puppy, he will have healthier teeth throughout his life.

IDENTIFICATION and Finding the Lost Dog

BY JUDY IBY

There are several ways of identifying your dog. The old standby is a collar with dog license, rabies, and ID tags. Unfortunately collars have a way of being separated from the dog and tags fall off. We're not suggesting you shouldn't use a collar and tags. If they stay intact and on the dog, they are the quickest way of identification.

For several years owners have been tattooing their dogs. Some tattoos use a number with a registry. Here lies the problem because there are several registries to check. If you wish to tattoo, use your social security number. The humane shelters have the means to trace it. It is usually done on the inside of the rear thigh. The area is first shaved and numbed. There is no pain, although a few dogs do not like the buzzing sound. Occasionally tattooing is not legible and needs to be redone.

The newest method of identification is microchipping. The microchip is a computer chip that is no larger than a grain of rice. The veterinarian implants it by injection between the shoulder blades. The dog feels no discomfort. If your dog is lost and picked up by the humane society, they can trace you by scanning the microchip, which has its own code. Microchip scanners are friendly to other brands of microchips and their registries. The microchip comes with a dog tag saying the dog

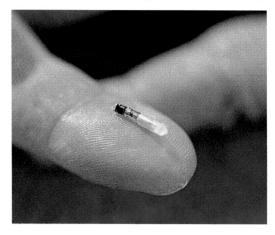

The newest method of identification is microchipping. The microchip is a computer chip no bigger than a grain of rice.

is microchipped. It is the safest way of identifying your dog.

FINDING THE LOST DOG

I am sure you will agree that there would be little worse than losing your dog. Responsible pet owners rarely lose their dogs. They do not let their dogs run free because they don't want harm to come to them. Not only that but in most, if not all, states there is a leash law.

Beware of fenced-in yards. They can be

For his safety, your Doberman Pinscher should wear a collar and identification tags at all times.

Always keep your dog on lead to prevent him from becoming separated from you.

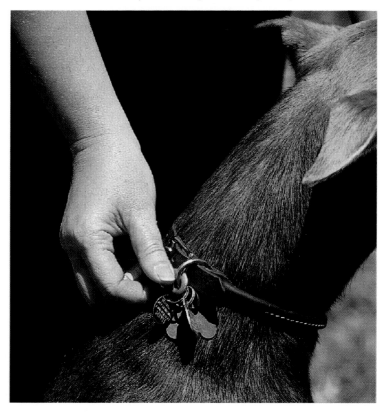

a hazard. Dogs find ways to escape either over or under the fence. Another fast exit is through the gate that perhaps the neighbor's child left unlocked.

Below is a list that hopefully will be of help to you if you need it. Remember don't give up, keep looking. Your dog is worth your efforts.

The Doberman is a large-sized breed, so make sure his enclosure is secure enough to hold him.

1. Contact your neighbors and put flyers with a photo on it in their mailboxes. Information you should include would be the dog's name, breed, sex, color, age, source of identification, when your dog was last seen and where, and your name and phone numbers. It may be helpful to say the dog needs medical care. Offer a *reward*.

2. Check all local shelters daily. It is also possible for your dog to be picked up away from home and end up in an out-of-the-way shelter. Check these too. Go in person. It is not good enough to call. Most shelters are limited on the time they can hold dogs then they are put up for adoption or euthanized. There is the possibility that your dog will not make it to the shelter for several days. Your dog could have been wandering or someone may have tried to keep him.

3. Notify all local veterinarians. Call and send flyers.

4. Call your breeder. Frequently breeders are contacted when one of their breed is found.

5. Contact the rescue group for your breed.

6. Contact local schools—children may have seen your dog.

7. Post flyers at the schools, groceries, gas stations, convenience stores, veterinary clinics, groomers and any other place that will allow them.

8. Advertise in the newspaper.

9. Advertise on the radio.

A fenced-in yard is necessary to keep your Doberman from wandering off.

TRAVELING with Your Dog

BY JUDY IBY

The earlier you start traveling with your new puppy or dog, the better. He needs to become accustomed to traveling. However, some dogs are nervous riders and become carsick easily. It is helpful if he starts with an empty stomach. Do not despair, as it will go better if you continue taking him with you on short fun rides. How would you feel if every time you rode in the car you stopped at the doctor's for an injection? You would soon dread that nasty car. Older dogs that tend to get carsick may have more of a problem adjusting to traveling. Those dogs that are having a serious problem may benefit from some medication prescribed by the veterinarian.

Do give your dog a chance to relieve himself before getting into the car. It is a good idea to be prepared for a clean up with a leash, paper towels, bag and terry cloth towel.

The safest place for your dog is in a fiberglass crate, although close confinement can promote carsickness in some dogs. If your dog is nervous you can try letting him ride on the seat next to you or in someone's lap.

An alternative to the crate would be to use a car harness made for dogs and/or a safety strap attached to the harness or collar. Whatever you do, do not let your dog ride in the back of a pickup truck unless he is securely tied on a very short lead. I've seen trucks stop quickly and, even though the dog was tied, it fell out and was dragged.

Another advantage of the crate is that it is a safe place to leave him if you need to run into the store. Otherwise you wouldn't be able to leave the windows down. Keep in mind that while many dogs are overly protective in their crates, this may not be enough to deter dognappers. In some states it is against the law to leave a dog in the car unattended.

Never leave a dog loose in the car wearing a collar and leash. More than one dog has killed himself by hanging. Do not let him put his head out an open window. Foreign debris can be blown into his eyes. When leaving your dog unattended in a car, consider the temperature. It can take less than five minutes to reach temperatures over 100 degrees Fahrenheit.

TRIPS

Perhaps you are taking a trip. Give consideration to what is best for your dog—traveling with you or boarding. When traveling by car, van or motor home, you need to think ahead about locking your vehicle. In all probability you have many valuables in the car and do not wish to leave it unlocked. Perhaps most valuable and not replaceable is your dog. Give thought to securing your vehicle and providing adequate ventilation for him. Another consideration for you when traveling with your dog is medical problems that may arise and little

Your Doberman won't have stay home alone as often if you accustom him to traveling. Truslove Quest For Donovan waits patiently for his master.

inconveniences, such as exposure to external parasites. Some areas of the country are quite flea infested. You may want to carry flea spray with you. This is even a good idea when staying in motels. Quite possibly you are not the only occupant of the room.

Unbelievably many motels and even hotels do allow canine guests, even some very first-class ones. Gaines Pet Foods Corporation publishes *Touring With Towser*, a directory of domestic hotels and motels that accommodate guests with dogs. Their address is Gaines TWT, PO Box 5700, Kankakee, IL, 60902. Call ahead to any motel that you may be considering and see if they accept pets. Sometimes it is necessary to pay a deposit against room damage. The management may feel reassured if you mention that your dog will be crated. If you do travel with your dog, take along plenty of baggies so that you can clean up after him. When we all do our share in cleaning up, we make it possible for motels to continue accepting our pets. As a matter of fact, you should practice cleaning up everywhere you take your dog.

The more your Doberman Pinscher travels with you, the more he will be willing to follow you anywhere.

Depending on where your are traveling, you may need an up-to-date health certificate issued by your veterinarian. It is good policy to take along your dog's medical information, which would include the name, address and phone number of your veterinarian, vaccination record, rabies certificate, and any medication he is taking.

Because they are such hardy and accommodating dogs, Dobermans enjoy vacationing in any climate. This nine-month-old gets his first taste of snow.

AIR TRAVEL

When traveling by air, you need to contact the airlines to check their policy. Usually you have to make arrangements up to a couple of weeks in advance for traveling with your dog. The airlines require your dog to travel in an airline approved fiberglass crate. Usually these can be purchased through the airlines but they are also readily available in most pet-supply stores. If your dog is not accustomed to a crate, then it is a good idea to get him acclimated to it before your trip. The day of the actual trip you should withhold water about one hour ahead of departure and no food for about 12 hours. The airlines generally have temperature restrictions, which do not allow pets to travel if it is either too cold or too hot. Frequently these restrictions are based on the temperatures at the departure and arrival airports. It's best to inquire about a health certificate. These usually need to be issued within ten days of departure. You should arrange for non-stop, direct flights and if a commuter plane should be involved, check to see if it will carry dogs. Some don't. The Humane Society of the United States has put together a tip sheet for airline traveling. You can receive a copy by sending a self-addressed stamped envelope to:

The Humane Society of the United States
Tip Sheet
2100 L Street NW
Washington, DC 20037.

Regulations differ for traveling outside of the country and are sometimes changed without notice. Well in advance you need to write or call the appropriate consulate or agricultural department for instructions. Some countries have lengthy quarantines (six months), and countries differ in their rabies vaccination requirements. For instance, it may have to be given at least 30 days ahead of your departure.

Do make sure your dog is wearing proper identification including your name, phone number and city. You never know when you might be in an accident and separated from your dog. Or your dog could be frightened and somehow manage to escape and run away.

Another suggestion would be to carry in-case-of-emergency instructions. These would include the address and phone number of a relative or friend, your veterinarian's name, address and phone number, and your dog's medical information.

BOARDING KENNELS

Perhaps you have decided that you need to board your dog. Your veterinarian can recommend a good boarding facility or possibly a pet sitter that will come to your house. It is customary for the boarding kennel to ask for proof of vaccination for the DHLPP, rabies and bordetella vaccine. The bordetella should have been given within six months of boarding. This is for your protection. If they do not ask for this proof I would not board at their kennel. Ask about flea control. Those dogs that suffer flea-bite allergy can get in trouble at a boarding kennel. Unfortunately boarding kennels are limited on how much they are able to do.

For more information on pet sitting, contact NAPPS:
National Association of Professional Pet Sitters
1200 G Street, NW
Suite 760
Washington, DC 20005.

Some pet clinics have technicians that pet sit and technicians that board clinic patients in their homes. This may be an alternative for you. Ask your veterinarian if they have an employee that can help you. There is a definite advantage of having a technician care for your dog, especially if your dog is on medication or is a senior citizen.

When you travel, bring your Doberman's favorite things with you, like his crate and his toys, to make him feel at home.

You can write for a copy of *Traveling With Your Pet* from ASPCA, Education Department, 441 E. 92nd Street, New York, NY 10128.

BEHAVIOR and Canine Communication

BY JUDY IBY

S tudies of the human/animal bond point out the importance of the unique relationships that exist between people and their pets. Those of us who share our lives with pets understand the special part they play through companionship, service and protection. For many, the pet/owner bond goes beyond simple companionship; pets are often considered members of the family. A leading pet food manufacturer recently conducted a nationwide survey of pet owners to gauge just how important pets were in their lives. Here's what they found:

Doberman Pinschers enrich the lives of their owners by being loving and faithful companions.

- 76 percent allow their pets to sleep on their beds
- 78 percent think of their pets as their children
- 84 percent display photos of their pets, mostly in their homes
- 84 percent think that their pets react to their own emotions
- 100 percent talk to their pets
- 97 percent think that their pets understand what they're saying

Are you surprised?

Senior citizens show more concern for their own eating habits when they have the responsibility of feeding a dog. Seeing that their dog is routinely exercised encourages the owner to think of schedules that otherwise may seem unimportant to the senior citizen. The older owner may be arthritic and feeling poorly but with responsibility for his dog he has a reason to get up and get moving. It is a big plus if his dog is an attention seeker who will demand such from his owner.

Over the last couple of decades, it has been shown that pets relieve the stress of those who lead busy lives. Owning a pet has been known to lessen the occurrence of heart attack and stroke.

Many single folks thrive on the companionship of a dog. Lifestyles are very different from a long time ago, and today

more individuals seek the single life. However, they receive fulfillment from owning a dog.

Most likely the majority of our dogs live in family environments. The companionship they provide is well worth the effort involved. In my opinion, every child should have the opportunity to have a family dog. Dogs teach responsibility through understanding their care, feelings and even respecting their life cycles. Frequently those children who have not been exposed to dogs grow up afraid of dogs, which isn't good. Dogs sense timidity and some will take advantage of the situation.

It is not unusual for the Doberman to adopt other animals. This Von Ryan Dobe took over as friend and protector of this young fawn.

Today more dogs are serving as service dogs. Since the origination of the Seeing Eye dogs years ago, we now have trained hearing dogs. Also dogs are trained to provide service for the handicapped and are able to

perform many different tasks for their owners. Search and Rescue dogs, with their handlers, are sent throughout the world to assist in recovery of disaster victims. They are life savers.

Therapy dogs are very popular with nursing homes, and some hospitals even allow them to visit. The inhabitants truly look forward to their visits. They wanted and were allowed to have visiting dogs in their beds to hold and love.

Nationally there is a Pet Awareness Week to educate students and others about the value and basic care of our pets. Many countries take an even greater interest in their pets than Americans do. In those countries the pets are allowed to accompany their owners into restaurants and shops, etc. In the U.S. this freedom is only available to our service dogs. Even so we think very highly of the human/ animal bond.

It has been found that spending time with a dog can reduce stress and improve the quality of life. Who can resist this sweet Doberman?

CANINE BEHAVIOR

Canine behavior problems are the number-one reason for pet owners to dispose of their dogs, either through new homes, humane shelters or euthanasia. Unfortunately there are too many owners who are unwilling to devote the necessary time to properly train their dogs. On the other hand, there are those who not only are concerned about inherited health problems but are also aware of the dog's mental stability.

You may realize that a breed and his group relatives (i.e., sporting, hounds, etc.) show tendencies to behavioral characteristics. An experienced breeder can acquaint you with his breed's personality. Unfortunately many breeds are labeled with poor temperaments when actually the breed as a whole is not affected but only a small percentage of individuals within the breed.

Inheritance and environment contribute to the dog's behavior. Some naïve people suggest inbreeding as the cause of bad temperaments. Inbreeding only results in poor behavior if the ancestors carry the trait. If there are excellent temperaments behind the dogs, then inbreeding will promote good temperaments in the offspring. Did you ever consider that inbreeding is what sets the characteristics of a breed? A purebred dog is the end result of inbreeding. This does not spare the mixed-breed dog from the same problems. Mixed-breed dogs frequently are the offspring of purebred dogs.

Not too many decades ago most of our dogs led a different lifestyle than what is prevalent today. Usually mom stayed home so the dog had human companionship and someone to discipline it if needed. Not much was expected from the dog. Today's mom works and everyone's life is at a much faster pace.

Thank you Easter Bunny! A whole nestful of HoMike Dobermans demonstrate the advantages of pack mentality.

The dog may have to adjust to being a "weekend" dog. The family is gone all day during the week, and the dog is left to his own devices for entertainment. Some dogs sleep all day waiting for their family to come home and others become wigwam wreckers if given the opportunity. Crates do ensure the safety

of the dog and the house. However, he could become a physically and emotionally cripple if he doesn't get enough exercise and attention. We still appreciate and want the companionship of our dogs although we

A crate will ensure your dog's safety when he is left unsupervised.

The way your Doberman Pinscher puppy interacts with his littermates can give you a key to his personality.

expect more from them. In many cases we tend to forget dogs are just that—*dogs* not human beings.

Socializing and Training

Many prospective puppy buyers lack experience regarding the proper socialization and training needed to develop the type of pet we all desire. In the first 18 months, training does take some work. It is easier to start proper training before there is a problem that needs to be corrected.

Dobermans are intelligent, athletic dogs that can be taught to excel at many different activities when properly trained.

The initial work begins with the breeder. The breeder should start socializing the puppy at five to six weeks of age and cannot let up. Human socializing is critical up through 12 weeks of age and likewise important during the following months. The litter should be left together during the first few weeks but it is necessary to separate them by ten weeks of age. Leaving them together after that time will increase competition for litter dominance. If puppies are not socialized with people by 12 weeks of age, they will be timid in later life.

The eight- to ten-week age period is a fearful time for puppies. They need to be handled very gently around children and adults. There should be no harsh discipline during this time. Starting at 14 weeks of age, the puppy begins the juvenile period, which ends when he reaches sexual maturity around six to 14 months of age. During the juvenile period he needs to be introduced to strangers (adults, children and other dogs) on the home property. At sexual maturity he will begin to bark at strangers and become more protective. Males start to lift their legs to urinate but if you desire you can inhibit this behavior by walking your boy on leash away from trees, shrubs, fences, etc.

The picture of loyalty and perseverance, Pearnperfect Frozen In Time awaits the arrival of her family.

Perhaps you are thinking about an older puppy. You need to inquire about the puppy's social experience. If he has lived in a kennel, he may have a hard time adjusting to people and environmental stimuli. Assuming he has had a good social upbringing, there are advantages to an older puppy.

Part of the joy of Doberman Pinscher ownership is the ability to take your dog on almost any kind of adventure.

Training includes puppy kindergarten and a minimum of one to two basic training classes. During these classes you will learn how to dominate your youngster. This is especially important if you own a large breed of dog. It is somewhat harder, if not nearly impossible, for some owners to be the Alpha figure when their dog towers over them. You will be taught how to properly restrain your dog. This concept is important. Again it puts you in the Alpha position. All dogs need to be restrained many times during their lives. Believe it or not, some of our worst offenders are the eight-week-old puppies that are brought to our clinic. They need to be gently restrained for a nail trim but the way they carry on you would think we were killing them. In comparison, their vaccination is a "piece of cake." When we ask dogs to do something that is not agreeable to them, then their worst comes out. Life will be easier for your dog if you expose him at a young age to the necessities of life—proper behavior and restraint.

Understanding the Dog's Language

Most authorities agree that the dog is a descendent of the wolf. The dog and wolf have similar traits. For instance both are pack oriented and prefer not to be isolated for long periods of time. Another characteristic is that the dog, like the wolf, looks to the leader—Alpha—for direction. Both the wolf and the dog communicate through body language, not only within their pack but with outsiders.

It's easy to read the body language of these two Truslove pups—they're exhausted!

Every pack has an Alpha figure. The dog looks to you, or should look to you, to be that leader. If your dog doesn't receive the proper training and guidance, he very well may replace you as Alpha. This would be a serious problem and is certainly a disservice to your dog.

Eye contact is one way the Alpha wolf keeps order within his pack. You are Alpha so you must establish eye contact with your puppy. Obviously your puppy will have to look at you. Practice eye contact even if you need to hold his head for five to ten seconds at a time. You can give him a treat as a reward. Make sure your eye contact is gentle and not threatening. Later, if he has been naughty, it is permissible to give him a long, penetrating look. There are some older dogs that never learned eye contact as puppies and cannot accept eye contact. You should avoid eye contact with these dogs since they feel threatened and will retaliate as such.

Body Language

The play bow, when the forequarters are down and the hindquarters are elevated, is an invitation to play. Puppies play fight, which helps them learn the acceptable limits of biting. This is necessary for later in their lives. Nevertheless, an owner may be falsely reassured by the playful nature of his dog's aggression. Playful aggression toward another dog or human may be an indication of serious aggression in the future. Owners should never play fight or play tug-of-war with any dog that is inclined to be dominant.

Signs of submission are:
1. Avoids eye contact.
2. Active submission—the dog crouches down, ears back and the tail is lowered.
3. Passive submission—the dog rolls on his side with his hindlegs in the air and frequently urinates.

The reluctance to part with toys when commanded may signal that a dog is not submissive to his owner. Establish yourself as boss early in your relationship with your Doberman.

Signs of dominance are:
1. Makes eye contact.
2. Stands with ears up, tail up and the hair raised on his neck.
3. Shows dominance over another dog by standing at right angles over it.

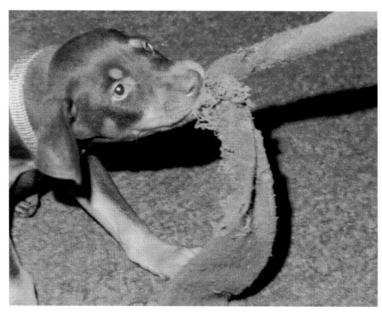

Dobermans get along very well in family situations—they are completely devoted to their "pack."

Dominant dogs tend to behave in characteristic ways such as:

1. The dog may be unwilling to move from his place (i.e., reluctant to give up the sofa if the owner wants to sit there).

2. He may not part with toys or objects in his mouth and may show possessiveness with his food bowl.

3. He may not respond quickly to commands.

4. He may be disagreeable for grooming and dislikes to be petted.

Dogs are popular because of their sociable nature. Those that have contact with humans during the first 12 weeks of life regard them as a member of their own species—their pack. All dogs have the potential for both dominant and submissive behavior. Only through experience and training do they learn to whom it is appropriate to show which behavior. Not all dogs are concerned with dominance but owners need to be aware of that potential. It is wise for the owner to establish his dominance early on.

A human can express dominance or submission toward a dog in the following ways:

1. Meeting the dog's gaze signals dominance. Averting the gaze signals submission. If the dog growls or threatens, averting the gaze is the first avoiding action to take—it may prevent attack. It is important to establish eye contact in the puppy. The older dog that has not been exposed to eye contact may see it as a threat and will not be willing to submit.

Off with the wash mitt! Just because this young Doberman is well trained does not mean she is not up for a few games of "keep away" with her owner.

2. Being taller than the dog signals dominance; being lower signals submission. This is why, when attempting to make friends with a strange dog or catch the runaway, one should kneel down to his level. Some owners see their dogs become dominant when allowed on the furniture or on the bed. Then he is at the owner's level.

3. An owner can gain dominance by ignoring all the dog's social initiatives. The owner pays attention to the dog only when he obeys a command.

No dog should be allowed to achieve dominant status over any adult or child. Ways of preventing are as follows:

1. Handle the puppy gently, especially during the three- to four-month period.
2. Let the children and adults handfeed him and teach him to take food without lunging or grabbing.
3. Do not allow him to chase children or joggers.
4. Do not allow him to jump on people or mount their legs. Even females may be inclined to mount. It is not only a male habit.
5. Do not allow him to growl for any reason.
6. Don't participate in wrestling or tug-of-war games.
7. Don't physically punish puppies for aggressive behavior. Restrain him from repeating the infraction and teach an alternative behavior. Dogs should earn everything

If a Doberman is properly socialized from the time he is a puppy, he should not exhibit fear when meeting different people or when in different surroundings.

they receive from their owners. This would include sitting to receive petting or treats, sitting before going out the door and sitting to receive the collar and leash. These types of exercises reinforce the owner's dominance.

Young children should never be left alone with a dog. It is important that children learn some basic obedience commands so they have some control over the dog. They will gain the respect of their dog.

FEAR

One of the most common problems dogs experience is being fearful. Some dogs are more afraid than others. On the lesser side, which is sometimes humorous to watch, dogs can be afraid of a strange object. They act silly when something is out of place in the house. We call his problem perceptive intelligence. He realizes the abnormal within his known environment. He does not react the same way in strange environments since he does not know what is normal.

On the more serious side is a fear of people. This can result in backing off, seeking his own space and saying "leave me alone" or it can result in an aggressive behavior that may lead to challenging the person. Respect that the dog wants to be left alone and give him time to come forward. If you approach the cornered dog, he may resort to snapping. If you leave him alone, he may decide to come forward, which should be rewarded with a treat.

Some dogs may initially be too fearful to take treats. In these cases it is helpful to make sure the dog hasn't eaten for about 24 hours. Being a little hungry encourages him to accept the treats, especially if they are of the "gourmet" variety.

Dogs can be afraid of numerous things, including loud noises and thunderstorms. Invariably the owner rewards (by comforting) the dog when it shows signs of fearfulness. When your dog is frightened, direct his attention to something else and act happy. Don't dwell on his fright.

AGGRESSION

Some different types of aggression are: predatory, defensive, dominance, possessive, protective, fear induced, noise provoked, "rage" syndrome (unprovoked aggression), maternal and aggression directed toward other dogs. Aggression is the most common behavioral problem encountered. Protective breeds are expected to be more aggressive than others but with the proper upbringing they can make very dependable companions. You need to be able to read your dog.

Many factors contribute to aggression including genetics and environment. An improper environment, which may include the living conditions, lack of social life, excessive punishment, being attacked or frightened by an aggressive dog, etc., can all influence a dog's behavior. Even spoiling him and giving too much praise may be detrimental. Isolation and the lack of human contact or exposure to frequent teasing by children or adults also can ruin a good dog.

Lack of direction, fear, or confusion lead to aggression in those dogs that are so inclined. Any obedience exercise, even the sit and down, can direct the dog and overcome fear and/or confusion. Every dog should learn these commands as a youngster, and there should be periodic reinforcement.

When a dog is showing signs of aggression, you should speak calmly (no screaming or hysterics) and firmly give a command that he understands, such as the sit. As soon as your dog obeys, you have assumed your dominant position. Aggression presents a problem because there may be danger to others. Sometimes it is an emotional issue. Owners may consciously or unconsciously encourage their dog's aggression.

"I didn't do it!" Even the best-trained Dobermans can get into mischief if not properly socialized. Other owners show responsibility by accepting the problem and taking measures to keep it under control. The owner is responsible for his dog's actions, and it is not wise to take a chance on someone being bitten,

155

especially a child. Euthanasia is the solution for some owners and in severe cases this may be the best choice. However, few dogs are that dangerous and very few are that much of a threat to their owners. If caution is exercised and professional help is gained early on, most cases can be controlled.

Even the most adorable of puppies can experience behavior problems. That is why it is important to be a firm and fair owner.

Some authorities recommend feeding a lower protein (less than 20 percent) diet. They believe this can aid in reducing aggression. If the dog loses weight, then vegetable oil can be added. Veterinarians and behaviorists are having some success with

If you teach your Doberman Pinscher puppy the ABC's of training, he will soon become a well-mannered companion.

pharmacology. In many cases treatment is possible and can improve the situation.

If you have done everything according to "the book" regarding training and socializing and are still having a behavior problem, don't procrastinate. It is important that the problem gets attention before it is out of hand. It is estimated that 20 percent of a veterinarian's time may be devoted to dealing with problems before they become so intolerable that the dog is separated from its home and owner. If your veterinarian isn't able to help, he should refer you to a behaviorist.

Barking

This is a habit that shouldn't be encouraged. Some owners desire their dog to bark so as to be a watchdog. Most dogs will bark when a stranger comes to the door.

The new puppy frequently barks or whines in the crate in his strange environment and the owner reinforces the puppy's bad behavior by going to him during the night. This is a no-no. Smack the top of the crate and say "quiet" in a loud, firm voice. The puppies don't like to hear the loud noise of the crate being banged. If the barking is sleep-interrupting, then the owner should take crate and pup to the bedroom for a few days until the puppy becomes adjusted to his new environment. Otherwise ignore the barking during the night.

Barking can be an inherited problem or a bad habit learned through the environment. It takes dedication to stop the barking. Attention should be paid to the cause of the barking. Does the dog seek attention, does he need to go out, is it feeding time, is it occurring when he is left alone, is it a protective bark, etc.? Overzealous barking is an inherited tendency. When barking presents a problem for you, try to stop it as soon as it begins.

There are electronic collars available that are supposed to curb barking. There are some disadvantages to to the collar. If the dog is barking out of excitement, punishment is not the appropriate treatment. Presumably there is the chance the collar could be activated by other stimuli and thereby punish the dog when it is not barking. Should you decide to use one, then you should seek help from a person with experience with that type of collar. Nevertheless the root of the problem needs to be investigated and corrected.

In extreme circumstances (usually when there is a problem with the neighbors), some people have resorted to having their dogs debarked. I caution you that the dog continues to bark but usually only a squeaking sound is heard. Frequently the vocal cords grow back. Probably the biggest concern is that the dog can be left with scar tissue which can narrow the opening to the trachea.

RESOURCES

Doberman Pinscher Club of America
Corresponding Secretary: Sam Burke
3288 Bert Kouns Loop
Shreveport, LA 71118
www.dpca.org

American Kennel Club
260 Madison Avenue
New York, New York 10016
or 5580 Centerview Drive
Raleigh, North Carolina 27606
919-233-3600
919-233-9767
www.akc.org

The United Kennel Club, Inc.
100 E. Kilgore Road
Kalamazoo, Michigan 49002-5584
616-343-9020
www.ukcdogs.com

The Kennel Club
1 Clarges Street
Picadilly, London WIY 8AB, England

Canadian Kennel Club
100-89 Skyway Avenue
Etobicoke, Ontario, Canada M9W6R4

INDEX